BE AWESOME!

BANISH BURNOUT:
Create Motivation
from the Inside Out

By Kristina Hallett, PhD, ABPP

Cover Design: Sally Wright Day

Editing: Maggie McReynolds

Author's photo courtesy of Sandra Costello,
Sandra Costello Photography

In the words of the Dalai Lama,
"The many factors which divide us are
actually much more superficial than those
we share...we are all equal concerning
our fundamental humanity."
This book is dedicated to all those
who continue to show compassion
and caring, treating others with respect
and dignity, despite the stormy waters
of life circumstances.

Table of Contents

Introduction

What do you most want in your life right now? Peace? Excitement? Time? To feel different? To feel better? To get to a place (or back to a place) of loving your job? Is it something external or something internal? Or maybe both? Whatever it is, there's a way forward. Even if it's an issue you've been struggling with for a long time.

This book is meant to provide guidance, a path through the wilderness that will lead you out of the woods and back home. It's based on concepts that are vital to living your best life, but they are concepts that we often put on the back burner or ignore altogether. This book is about how we let go of stress, move away from burnout, and feel energized and motivated from the inside out. *BE AWESOME!* is based in practical awareness and scientific knowledge. If you want to start doing instead of wishing, read this book!

A huge number of people (75 percent of people polled!) report experiencing significant levels of stress, with stress having a definite impact on their sense of happiness and well-being. Workload and work-family balance are two of the top three areas of stress. This isn't a new problem. The American Psychological Association has been conducting the nationwide survey Stress in America™ since 2007. In 2017, 45 percent of Americans reported stress-induced sleep loss in the previous month. One-third reported feeling nervous/anxious, irritable, or angry, along with fatigue, due to their stress.

When we can #BeAWESOME, we are able to do *what* we love, with *whom* we love, in a balanced way without stress or guilt. The AWESOME process covers concrete steps to remove limitations and repurpose energy to maximize productivity and eliminate burnout. *Be AWESOME!* provides tools for busy professionals to reclaim their passions and revive their drive and motivation while maintaining productive, fulfilling work and home lives.

Burnout is not a one-time experience, and it's not limited to work situations. Burnout happens when we have gone from excited (about life, work, the future) to feeling continuously exhausted and feeling that we're struggling. It may be hard to get up in the morning, and you may spend the day looking forward to dropping back into bed at night, barely noticing what happens during the day. You may find yourself more irritable, more easily frustrated or annoyed, more emotional, or even numb, barely feeling any emotion at all. You may be restless or lethargic, finding it difficult to concentrate or find satisfaction. Physical ailments and illness often accompany burnout, including headaches, stomachaches, colds, and muscle aches and pains. Sometimes it is just an overall feeling of being "off" without any known reason.

Burnout impairs our relationships—both with ourselves and with those around us. We become less productive (it's hard to stay on task when we constantly feel on edge). And we start to see things as difficult, decreasing our feeling of motivation and ability to act. We may withdraw from others, desperately seeking peace, while craving connection and understanding.

Several years ago, I was in this place. (That wasn't the only time, but it was a biggie.) I was working at a job that required an hour commute each way, then racing from my day job to spend time at my private practice in the evenings. I was moving as fast as I could, and I felt like I was losing ground every day. I *hated* the commute, and usually spent most of my driving time complaining on the phone to whoever was willing to talk with me. Of course, this just reinforced my unhappiness and dissatisfaction. I liked the actual work I did, but getting to work started my day from a deficit. This pattern continued to escalate. I had less energy to give to my clients, and virtually no energy left for my family. Taking care of myself was absolutely not on the agenda. Who has time for self-care when all you want to do is crawl into bed and hope tomorrow is marginally better than today?

In classic I'm-burned-out-but-I-don't-know-it fashion, I began to withdraw from my friends and family. Social media was too depressing (everyone else seemed to be having a wonderful life, unlike me) and I didn't have anything to say. Returning texts and making phone calls felt like *way* too much work, and I didn't want to be a downer. I wasn't exercising, and let's just say my daily diet wasn't anything to recommend. In fact, "simple and mindless" is probably the nicest thing I could say about my eating habits back then. Sleep was a mixed bag, since falling asleep was a nightly challenge and I woke up every morning ready to go back to sleep before I'd thrown off the covers. All my love was saved for the snooze button—those precious eight more minutes before I had to face the day were like gold.

Emotionally, I just felt numb. There was no sparkle, no excitement, and no feelings of happiness or satisfaction. This was worse than the hamster on a wheel. This was panting on a treadmill, and every breath taking me closer to falling off the edge. I knew there was a problem, but I did not have the energy or awareness to figure it out. And all of this was made exponentially worse by the guilt I felt at falling behind in every area of my life. My internal self-critic was the only lively part of me. She was in overdrive, detailing with excruciating precision everything I wasn't doing and how much worse things could get. Confidence was low, peace was non-existent, and I knew I *should* start on the long list of changes to make things better, but wishing didn't *bring motivation*.

That's when *BE AWESOME!* was born, out of desperation, distress, and a desire for something *more*. I remember driving on my morning commute (not on the phone because I had worn out my friends and family with my unhappiness and negativity). Traffic had just started moving after the daily snarl and delay, and I was headed over a bridge, accelerating to try and get to work on time. I'm not sure what came over me, but I said out loud, "Ok, Universe, I'm ready. Bring it on. Because this just isn't working for me anymore."

Truthfully, I felt foolish as I was speaking — who was I talking to, and what did I really think was going to happen? Then I was scared … was it safe to taunt the Universe? Would things get worse? This lasted about two minutes, and then I shrugged it off. I had another day to get through, and the commute home through traffic to face. Bedtime was at least 15 hours away, and I would need several cups of coffee and all my determination to last until then.

I wish I could tell you that, from the moment of my challenge/plea to the Universe, everything changed. That would be a lie. But something shifted, the tiniest bit. I kept replaying that moment in my mind, slowly becoming aware of the degree to which I had stepped out of my own life. I was running on fumes and autopilot, and I needed to re-fuel fast. I wasn't at the point of out-of-control-careening-down-the-mountain-without-brakes (yet), but I wasn't far away.

I knew I had to stop wishing and start doing and take charge. Somehow. Right away. I started with the concepts of what would become the beginnings of my AWESOME program: *awareness* and *authenticity* – acknowledging how I felt, where I was stuck, and reviewing who I wanted to be. I'd been a fan of author and social researcher Brené Brown from her first book, *I Thought It Was Just Me*, so *wholehearted* was an easy concept to identify on my wish list. The next part of the AWESOME process, *willingness,* took a lot more courage and internal convincing. *Engagement* and *connection* were major missing pieces. Starting to reach out was harder than I thought, mostly because I wasn't comfortable asking for and receiving help. *Spirituality* and *energy* went hand in hand as I looked for some meaning and understanding of how to move forward. As you can imagine, this required *openness* and *forgiveness*, confronting and moving through self-doubt, and accepting responsibility for the choices that had brought me to this point, honoring the successes I had ignored, and embracing the knowledge acquired from where I had failed. *Mindfulness* was the actual path to *motivation,* living in the present as fully as I could and increasing my ability to try new perspectives and behaviors. As I put each of these together, the AWESOME process was born.

Throughout *BE AWESOME!* you will hear stories from my life and from those I have coached. You will see the pitfalls and the triumphs, the scientific and the heart-driven spiritual, the necessary elements to:
- Have the time, energy, and motivation to meet your goals.
- Do more of what you love, with whom you love, without guilt.
- Drop the shoulds and discover new opportunities for success.
- Take the risks you never imagined.

- Let go of suffering, stress, and anxiety, and experience confidence, peace, and joy.

My hope for you is that this will make your awakening and progress faster and easier than my journey. While our situations are not exactly the same (each of us is unique!), I hope you will benefit from the information in this book, applying the knowledge and techniques that have worked so well for so many. It's time for *you* to own your AWESOME!

Chapter 1

The Path to Being Awesome

Warning: if you hang out with me too long,
I'll brainwash you into believing in yourself
and knowing you can achieve anything.
— **Anonymous**

On a call to discuss coaching, Susan told me, "I love my work, but I feel like I'm drowning. I'm so tired from working all the time. I don't like how I look, how I feel … and I can't get motivated to do anything different. I KNOW what to do … I'm just not doing it. I feel so guilty, because I know it's up to me. But it's not getting any better—it keeps getting worse."

Can you relate to Susan's situation? Have you been in that place of stagnation? Or feeling paralyzed? If you have, you know it's not fun. And what's even worse is that you can't claim ignorance. Because you already know that what's holding you back is inside YOU. That's exactly what makes this so awful and unbearable. You are plagued by guilt about *not doing*. You can't use the rationale of, "Oh, this is such a complex issue I can't unravel the strands to find a starting point." I mean, you absolutely *know* the right answer. You could repeat it in your sleep. In fact, you've dreamt about this, more than once. You've had the conversation a multitude of times, with your girlfriends, your spouse or partner. You've even had this conversation with your kids. It's so simple, right? Get off the couch, start working out, stop eating unhealthy foods, make time for vacation. Even Nike tells you: "Just do it." What's the problem?

Chances are that, if you're reading this book, you share a few common characteristics with Susan (and me, and so many other women!). It's likely that you are a high-performing, achievement-oriented, goal-driven, and successful professional woman. You've worked hard for your success and may have reached certain milestones earlier than usual, based on your intelligence, drive, and desire to do well. Some might call you a workaholic or a perfectionist. If you've heard those terms, you may have also heard an inner voice saying something like, "What's wrong with that? Look how far I've gotten. None of this would have happened if I didn't work long and hard." Or perhaps it's something like, "I believe in doing my best and continually striving for excellence."

You have been a goal-setter and *achiever*. You derive significant personal satisfaction from your professional life. You see your work product as a reflection of your degree of professionalism and competency, and you are passionate about doing your best. There are times when you would love to shift some of the mantle of responsibility to others, but your commitment to excellence makes this difficult. You're afraid that something will go wrong, and so you tend to take on and do more than your fair share. This may also be true at home, where your practice of nonstop juggling has resulted in you being planner, gift-buyer, organizer, and cheerleader, in addition to regular household duties.

You may have striven for high grades in high school and college. You likely want your performance evaluation to be at the highest level and have a hard time accepting any lesser ratings with equanimity. At some point you felt your physical size and condition was "acceptable," although that's not true at present (even though your friends and loved ones tell you that you're being too hard on yourself). You *know* you're not making healthy choices in eating, sleeping, or exercising, but all the self-recrimination isn't making a difference — it's just increasing your overall feeling of guilt. You're frustrated with yourself for getting into this position, and even more upset that you're not making changes. You feel powerless to enact the changes that you already know are needed and feel increasingly anxious that the problem is continuing (and maybe worsening). And on top of all that, there's a big discrepancy between what you see as your problems and issues and what those around you say. You get a lot of feedback from your friends and loved ones that you're "awesome." While you appreciate the sentiment, it doesn't sit well with you. It may feel like another obligation or expectation to live up to (as if you didn't already have enough of those in your own head). Or it may just seem false — that if they really knew what you think and how you feel, you certainly wouldn't be described as awesome. You know you're not terrible, but on the "awesome scale" of 0-100, you're falling far short of your self-required 95+. (And secretly, you're always trying to get to 100 and usually disappointed in yourself when that doesn't happen.)

Why are so many women in this exact same position? Why do we continue to see professional women struggling with self-esteem and self-care? We know *I don't have the time* doesn't hold water as the catch-all reason for continuing our behavior, and yet we continue to say this to ourselves. We read books, attend seminars, and go to classes on living healthy. We go to hypnotists, therapists, and our medical doctors. We may have tried acupuncture, or group programs, or good, old-fashioned willpower. And yet at the end of the day, women are struggling to find the time and get motivated to take care of themselves.

It's certainly not a lack of information. Television, radio, magazines, and social media all remind us multiple times a day that we need to start doing something to help ourselves. This isn't new. In a sample of two hours of television during a random weeknight, I saw three commercials related to food and weight loss, and about five commercials related to having "the good life." There's a clear message that self-esteem and positive self-image go hand in hand with being healthy, in shape, and having the things that reflect success (fancy car, jewelry from Jared, vacation trips to exotic locations). And of course, there's research to support the impact of marketing on self-perception.

Given that we know the problem ("I'm not taking care of myself in a healthy manner"), and we know the solution ("Make time to move my body, eat well, and get enough sleep"), then what's the issue? What's perpetuating the cycle of working too much, then coming home and collapsing in front of the television? Grabbing whatever food is handiest, and later dragging ourselves to bed, still worrying about the next day, all the while berating ourselves for not doing *something* to change the pattern?

Motivation can be awfully hard to come by after a long day at work, followed by driving home through traffic, knowing that there's still more to do when you get home. More emails to read and answer, more problems to solve, more planning to make sure that tomorrow goes as well as possible. And it's complicated, because you really love your work. You've built your career and worked long hours juggling impossible numbers of responsibilities to get where you are, and you're proud of that—as you should be! It just doesn't seem quite as easy as it should be. Perhaps you've started wondering if you're getting too old to keep going at this pace. Or bemoaning the loss of youthful vigor and the ability to feel (and be) productive on minimal sleep.

You just want a few minutes to relax and unwind. Yet that sets off the cycle of *I should* and *I can't*, of *I need to* and *I don't feel like it*. The repetitive chant of "nothing will change if I don't do it, but I'm not in the mood, so I'll do it tomorrow." And not only does tomorrow repeat the pattern, but all along you feel bad. Upset with yourself for *not doing*, feeling guilty for not making the *right* choice, and watching your mood and motivation slowly swirl down the drain. And because you're an overachiever in all things, you are so busy giving yourself a hard time about what you're *not doing*, that you also miss out on the benefits of relaxing on the couch.

We tend to think of motivation as the inner drive to get something done (or at least started), based on a combination of knowing what step to take and desired outcome. We imagine that it's *a state of being*, a feeling that will spark us into working harder and longer, and accomplishing goals. We treat motivation as if it's both the flame and the wick. And, given that, we try to increase the amount of motivation we feel as a means of spurring progress forward. And yet, commitment is really the wick, and taking present action is the flame. The feeling of motivation is more a *reflection* of the degree of interest and commitment we have in something, *rather than a direct measure* of our likelihood of actionable behavior and success.

We've gotten used to defining motivation as a feeling that's necessary: required for us to begin a new behavior or maintain a set of pre-existing behaviors. If you want to achieve a particular goal, it's certainly helpful to feel motivated. However, it is still possible for you to move forward without the feeling of motivation. That's where making a commitment comes in. We can get so caught up in our thoughts — "I don't feel like it," "I'm not in the mood," "It's too hard" — that we stop taking action. *Committing* to taking action and then *taking* an action start the ball rolling (even when you're not *feeling like it*).

Generally, the first step is the hardest, so it can be helpful to start with small actions. Try standing up for a minute, take a walk to the bathroom and back, and maybe take a few deep breaths. Those are all *actions,* and a little movement can set you rolling down the track. Once you get moving, it's much easier to keep going. Ultimately, your success in taking action results in the feeling of motivation. We will talk more about motivation later in the book, but for now keep in mind the distinction between wanting an outcome and feeling interested or excited about acting.

Let's go back to Susan. When she came to me for coaching, it was as if there were two separate women. There was the (outwardly) highly competent, successful, strong, and motivated leader. She worked in technology and had made major advancements in what was traditionally a male-dominated profession. And there was the (inwardly) self-critical, overworking, guilt-ridden, and anxious woman who felt she never did enough and was never good enough no matter how much she accomplished. This aspect of Susan saw her *failure* in motivation as a reflection of weakness and lack of value. And sadly,

Susan was by no means the first woman to present in this fashion. In fact, the majority of my 25 years of psychology and coaching practice has been spent with women whose story is similar to Susan's. I was one of those women myself (I'll share some of that story in the next chapter), and I still have times of struggle and self-doubt.

The good news is that we are slowly becoming a little more accepting of the need to acknowledge and address this issue. Multiple writers and researchers are talking about self-esteem and value (think Brené Brown, Amy Cuddy, Jen Sincero). It is your time—the time to stop feeling guilt, stop waiting for the feeling of "readiness" or motivation, and start taking charge of being AWESOME for yourself. It is time to develop a different type of self-confidence that is based on who you are: the fullest, most imperfect, and most human version of you. That's what this book is about—the roadmap for you to follow in order to ditch the guilt, and, as CEO of you, stop wishing and start taking action.

Chapter 2

Setting the Stage

*She made a promise to herself
to hold her own well-being sacred.*
— **Anonymous**

I used to joke that I was "always number 2" (making the kind of face that suggested human waste in addition to the actual number). I would say this as if it was humorous, when internally it was a measure of how bad I felt at not being *good enough*. No matter what achievement I reached, there was always someone who was doing more, doing better, reaching heights that I hadn't even considered. And every time I made the comparison, I felt a little more like number 2 (the kind on the bottom of your shoe that makes you wrinkle your nose in disgust and hop on one foot toward the back door and a paper towel).

What is sad about my self-assessment is that by all external measures, I had no evidence to support my belief. By external measures I was *good enough*, despite not feeling like it. Even when I didn't get my first choice at something, it was usually a blessing in disguise. Of course, we never recognize a blessing until much later (that's why it's *in disguise*). Nonetheless, my experiences were in line with what you would expect for a professional woman. Successes, setbacks, and periods of stability (and some stagnation) were the signposts along my career and personal path. But like so many other women, what stood out to me were the incidents of *not good enough*. And it only took one little setback to overshadow multiple experiences of positivity and success.

A little background about me.

For many years, I did well from an intellectual standpoint, but I had a limited sense of connection between mind and body, and virtually no spiritual connection at all. I had positive relationships with others, but fear of being *not good enough* held me back in a myriad of ways. I focused on learning, academics, and outward markers of achievement. I went to college and then to graduate school, earning my PhD in Clinical Psychology. I was (and am) fascinated by the way people think and interact. In many ways, this was born of my own (very critical) process of introspection. I felt a huge disconnect at the most fundamental level between what I was able to do and who I was. And being a good student, and then a good worker, created and perpetuated my sense of value through accomplishment.

Many of us are molded from our earliest years in school to place value on grades, sports, and other external areas that allow us to earn accolades for *doing well* rather than *living well*. Of course, that's not to say there's no value placed on behavior. I was certainly held to standards of citizenship, morality, and other character traits, although rarely did my school environment include a focus on confidence, self-esteem, or self-care.

Family values included treating others kindly, being fair, and working hard to achieve predetermined goals/ outcomes. But the focus was more on achievement than on integrated, internal development and acceptance of myself as a fallible human being.

Even though I knew I was human, there was still the sense that if I worked hard enough, I could somehow create a life that was continuously positive and fair and that would allow me to reach the goal of *happiness* as an end-state. (I'm not saying this was actually told to me—but it's certainly how I internalized and took to heart my perceptions of other people's standards). However, happiness as an end state is just not possible. Life isn't fair. We all have ups and downs—some of us far more profoundly than others. It's an ocean ride during which the waves are never completely calm and a storm can arise seemingly out of nowhere, tossing us around in unexpected ways. While we have control over the choices we make, we don't necessarily have control over the situations we encounter. And sometimes hard work doesn't result in the outcome we want.

When our sense of value is based on what we achieve or on specific outcomes we accomplish, rather than on who we are and how we live, we are setting ourselves up for a big fall. Because life is like the game Chutes and Ladders: we will *slide backwards* and encounter adversity. What allows us to keep going, to surmount and surpass the challenges, is a resilience born of getting in touch with and accepting our deepest, most human self. It's when we let go of the idea of perfection (one of the most damaging mythical concepts I know) and start to value our imperfections and our actual experiences, that we begin to come alive. When we honor and embrace our flawed, human self, we can truly connect with others.

During my years of living as a single mom, I was completely focused on providing my daughter with everything I *thought* she needed. I worked a crazy schedule, using any time she was with her father or in activities to add in extra work. I didn't want her to see herself as *less than* because she didn't have two parents at home. I would stay up late to catch up on emails and office work, along with laundry, cleaning, preparing lunches, and baking cookies for a class event. I wasn't able to be a room mother or participate in the PTO — all the meetings happened while I was at work. Instead, I agreed to lead her Girl Scout troop, since that was the only way I could manage to make the schedule work. We held the meetings at our house, and drop-off and pick-up was my only contact with other adults outside of work. There were a lot of things I couldn't get to (it's true — my lawn was cut but not beautiful, I had to draw the line somewhere!), but I did my best to be fully present during our time together. We made games out of chores and spent every Saturday morning at the library (one of the few places I felt some moments of peace and quiet).

Looking back, I know I did the best I could with what I had. But at the time, I constantly felt that I wasn't doing *enough* — not enough for my daughter, not enough for work, and definitely not enough for me. It felt selfish to even consider wanting time for myself — there was always so much to do and so little time.

Then I was laid off. My job as Director of Children's Services for a psychiatric hospital was eliminated, and I was unemployed. Happiness? No way! I felt like a total failure. Not only was money really tight, but I had lost the job that provided me with the external validation I relied on. I was responsible for my daughter, our house, our dogs. It was terrifying. Even worse, I felt like I had lost my footing, my certainty that I was a valued employee and could *make it all work*. I floundered internally while I did all the right things. I applied for jobs, went on interviews, met with a career counselor, and tried to keep our life as calm as possible. It was only at night that the panic would set in, intensified by my feelings of failure, self-doubt, and fear. I knew I was lucky. I knew that I had a degree that was marketable and that I would find work (I did), but at the time it was hard to stay positive and not take it as a personal indictment of my worth. Although I was assured it was a *business decision* and not reflective of my skills or value, that is not how it felt. All my training and knowledge, my objectivity and compassion, didn't seem to apply when I was the one floundering,

Although I'm trained as a clinical psychologist and I've spent decades helping others, my personal journey has had pitfalls, twists, and turns just like everyone else. There have been moments when I could clearly see all that's wonderful and fortunate. And there have been many more moments when all the helpful advice and support that I've given to others hasn't seemed to apply to *me*. Sure, everyone encounters obstacles, but somehow when it's your own life, it's much harder to be caring and compassionate (and objective!). So often, I didn't recognize the gifts in my experiences, just the strains and stressors. I struggled to see myself as a person of worth in my own right, separate from what I might achieve or do for others. My sense of personal value came primarily from what I *achieved,* rather than who I *was*. I was focusing on self-improvement through achievement, but the reality was the complete opposite. This is the path away from the self: away from self-confidence, self-love, self-acceptance, and self-worth. Instead, it's the super-highway to *not good enough*, with stops along the way for fear, distress, and doubt.

Getting laid off hit me harder than getting divorced. I'd created a story for myself that divorcing was in the best interests of my daughter, and the means of giving her the life she deserved. I saw divorce as necessary to providing the kind of environment and role modeling that she needed. Truthfully, I just stuffed my feelings of failure and *not good enough* deep inside, covered over by the narrative of being a strong, positive influence for my daughter.

When I was laid off, it all bubbled up. As I struggled with intense feelings of unworthiness and overwhelming fear, I started to hear an internal voice that said, "First you failed at marriage, now you lost your job—what's next? What kind of role model; what kind of mother are you?" It took time, work, and a lot more stumbling around before I began to lay down a solid foundation of self-esteem, and even longer until I began to actively practice self-care and self-love.

If you've read my first book, *Own Best Friend: Eight Steps to a Life of Purpose, Passion, and Ease*, then you're already familiar with the EMPOWERS process and a number of examples from my life—times when I didn't act for fear of someone else's opinion; times when I took on too much, for too long, because I felt I *should*; times that I embraced being a multitasking workaholic as evidence of my worthiness. And you learned how I discovered that the missing piece in my life revolved around being my #ownbestfriend (fits nicely with the title, right?).

The EMPOWERS process is about the foundational practices that lead us to be our #ownbestfriend. EMPOWERS as an acronym stands for:

    E – Enhance Your Energy
    M – Make More Time
    P – Practice Perspective
    O – Own Your Best Self
    W – Wake Up Your Inner Rockstar
    E – Envision Your Purpose
    R – Release the Blocks and Go for It
    S – Shine Your Light Brightly

Each of the steps in EMPOWERS is a separate chapter with exercises (simple, short practices) that will help you incorporate the central theme into your daily life. I'm a fan of small actions that cumulatively lead to large impact. In fact, that's the miracle of neuroplasticity. We now know that an "old dog *can* learn new tricks," and that happens through re-wiring our brains. We create new neural pathways by consistently repeating small actions and exercises, resulting in a new outlook and fuller potential (living with purpose, passion, and ease). Frankly, that's a lot more fun than staying stuck or spiraling downhill.

Which leads me to *BE AWESOME*. This book is a deeper look at the concepts and underlying belief in both knowing about being your own best friend and putting that into practice. #BeAWESOME is about taking your self-confidence to the next level, and moving into a place of freedom, awareness, and appreciation for who you *really* are. It's a whole new lease on life, where perfection no longer rules the roost, and we embrace failure as opportunity, and evidence that we are living fully. *BE AWESOME!* is about choice, risk, vulnerability, and embracing reasonable and realistic standards (instead of expecting more from ourselves than anyone else). It's how we honor and integrate mind, body, and spirit, and it's what allows us to be of most service to others. While *Own Best Friend* and EMPOWERS detail a lot of actions (stop multitasking; start saying no; finding ways to rest and relax; learning and utilizing personal strengths; using breathing, meditation and mindfulness), *BE AWESOME!* is a deeper, internal process. It's about delving into the underworld of our self-perception, bringing to the surface the anchors and wreckage that have weighed us down, and then allowing these shadow-parts to be just a portion of our accepted, whole self.

BE AWESOME reflects my personal journey, the process, and the knowledge gained from countless women I've worked with in psychotherapy, coaching, and supervision. I knew that the experiences I went through and encountered with my therapy and coaching clients were not unique. What is striking to me, across all the women I have known and worked with, is the huge discrepancy between how they see themselves as compared to how the world sees them.

All but one of the women described herself as less accomplished or *awesome* than what she imagined would be the description by those who know and love her.

Here's what some of the women I spoke to said:

"Other people tell me they think I'm awesome—I just don't see it. It's because they aren't in my head. They don't see what I feel inside."

"I'm working on being awesome, but it's hard. I don't give myself enough credit. I get stuck in my comfort zone."

"I know people who are awesome. I don't see myself that way. I guess I'm pretty self-critical, but I don't know how to stop."

"I find that I don't take risks because I'm afraid of being judged. I want to accept myself for who I am—feel good enough without feeling like I need to be someone else."

And every time the rationale was the same—some version of, "They are being kind because they care about me. They don't know all my faults and failures. If they did, they would not think I'm awesome at all." Each of these women was highly accomplished in her own right. Had overcome obstacles, set and achieved goals (personally and professionally), and still had struggled with repeatedly climbing the mountain of self-doubt.

It became abundantly clear that vulnerability—including vulnerability with ourselves (otherwise known as awareness, authenticity—two tenets of the AWE-

SOME process — and honesty) — was the first step toward permanently effecting a change in our self-perception. Remember that "permanently," in this context, means significantly shorter duration, frequency, and intensity of periods of fear, self-doubt, guilt, and feeling *not good enough*. As humans, we are always going to encounter situations that are challenging and prompt reactivity. Our goal is to return to the feeling of freedom and safety as soon as possible, not to do the impossible and avoid those situations altogether.

One of my coaching clients, Tanya, was so paralyzed by her fear of *screwing up* that she didn't want to try anything new or anything she thought she might not do perfectly. As you can imagine, it didn't start out too badly. Not going skiing or snowboarding didn't really impact her life. From Tanya's perspective, she didn't like the cold, so her refusal to join friends on the slopes wasn't about fear. It reflected her good boundaries by saying no. While it was important for Tanya to learn when and how to effectively limit her expectations of herself and those of others, her restrictive responses seemed to backfire. Tanya began to stay away more and more from activities that might be *hard* or that brought up any feelings of uncertainty or incompetency. Slowly, her areas of confidence and competence began to shrink, until work was her only area of perceived value. And in response, Tanya did more and more at work to demonstrate her value and to connect with those feelings of accomplishment and connection that were missing.

How do you imagine this worked for her? As you might guess, she became more stressed, more tired, and more irritable. And even worse (from her perspective), she became less productive at work. Tanya's personal standards and expectations were high, much higher than the standards and expectations she held for others. And as a result, she created a situation in which she was always falling short of what she felt she should achieve. As with any self-perpetuating cycle, this did not work to her benefit. Instead, she would work harder and do more, becoming increasingly discouraged and disheartened that she was falling further and further behind. Over time, her anxiety about not meeting her personal standards continued to grow, leading her to (you guessed it) work harder and do more. There was less and less time for rest and relaxation, until eventually she was at the point of burnout—from a career and profession that she loved and wanted to continue. When we met, Tanya knew that her approach wasn't working and that something needed to change *fast*. Enter the AWESOME process, transforming guilt, fear, and anxiety into an attainable practice of self-awareness that supports and maintains motivation, happiness, and fulfillment.

This is not to say you can't get there on your own. In fact, several of the women I interviewed, as well as others I personally know, got to #BeAWESOME well before this book was written. There are always alternatives, and there's no one "right" way for everyone. However, I'm sharing the AWESOME process because I want you to live your best life, and to start doing so in a way that's faster, easier and more fun than the path I took.

For me, the path from worthiness through accomplishment to feeling awesome about *who I am*, was a slow and roundabout journey. While I am most often in that place today, there are still numerous occasions that challenge my beliefs, at least temporarily. The difference is that the times of doubt and difficulty are fewer, don't last as long, and are (generally) less intense. As we go through the AWESOME process, I will share examples from my journey and the experiences of other women who have walked the same path.

This book is a testament to women's stories of moving forward and beyond perfection and the fear of *not being enough*. Through the AWESOME process, Tanya (and so many other women) have come to realize that it is our self-imposed standards that prevent us from achieving our highest potential, rather than lifting us up.

Chapter 3

The AWESOME Process

I welcome transformation. I welcome
growth. I welcome abundance.
I know what I need.
I AM READY.
— **Alberto Villoldo**

Welcome to #BeAWESOME — transforming guilt, fear, and anxiety into an attainable (and sustainable) practice of self-awareness and acceptance that supports and maintains motivation, happiness, and fulfillment. The AWESOME process is the ***simple, not easy*** means by which we own our real self, flaws, and fabulousness alike. *Simple, not easy* is the reality of implementing change that affects us at the deepest level. So often the solution to an issue seems deceptively simple. A clear choice between taking one action or another — between acting or choosing not to act. This was the concept behind "Just Say No" in the War on Drugs.

Based on the erroneous idea that because an action is simple, it should be easy to accomplish.

This couldn't be further from the truth. *Simple, not easy* is rooted in the acknowledgment that knowing what to do doesn't directly translate into taking action. Knowing what to do is about information. Acting on our knowledge is something we associate with the feeling of motivation. And then there's guilt. Guilt comes from the *I shoulds,* deriving from our expectations of ourselves as needing to be more, do more, achieve more. The *I shoulds* usually result from some version of "I'm not good enough unless…"

How do you define awesome? The dictionary says, "extremely good; excellent," listing synonyms including breathtaking, awe-inspiring, magnificent, wonderful, amazing, stunning, and impressive (among others). Is that how you see yourself? I'm guessing that's generally not how you picture yourself, at least internally. I hope that you do, but my decades of experiences working with women suggest that's not likely. However, I am certain that along the way you have been told by friends and loved ones, perhaps frequently, that "you are awesome." What is it that they have seen that you don't recognize in yourself? And wouldn't it be fantastic to *actually feel worthy* of being awesome?

Despite your skepticism (I can perfectly picture your rolling eyes, raised brows, and scrunched-up nose as you read the previous paragraph), the goal of this book is to provide you the means by which to live, and feel, awesome. To be in a place where your internal determination, and the assessment of others, are both positive and closely match each other. As mentioned, the internal state of AWESOME takes practice. It's a deceptively simple, yet in practice quite challenging, course of action. It's not physically grueling or demanding, although from an emotional perspective it does require fortitude and commitment.

And #AWESOME is achievable for YOU, no matter who you are or where you start, as long as you keep practicing. It's also not a stable state, meaning that, as life continues to hand you lemons or mountains, you will have times when you falter and question yourself. It's unavoidable. But through using the AWESOME process, you will increase your resilience, and even develop a different perspective on how you see challenges and failure.

The seven areas, (or steps, for simplicity's sake) of the AWESOME process are the primary tools for moving into the sense of #AWESOME that have been successful for me, and for the many women I have worked with. You will hear stories from Susan, Tanya, Anne, Margaret, Ellen, Mary, and me, as well as comments and quotes from the generous women who participated in interviews as part of the book writing process. Here's a brief overview of the steps of the AWESOME process. We will look at each of these in more detail in the coming chapters.

A—Awareness, Authenticity, Accountability

Naturally, we have to start at the beginning. That means we must develop an *Awareness* of how we view ourselves, from a compassionate yet objective perspective. I know that you may *think* you already do this, but unless you see yourself as being as amazingly wonderful as your friends and loved ones see you, you've missed the mark. Here's the thing — when people who know you well tell you that you're *Awesome*, they're not lying. They aren't just saying something to make you feel better or to cheer you up. They are sharing how *they see you.* And it's not because they think you are "perfect." It is because they have a view of you that isn't tainted by self-doubt.

This is where *Authenticity* comes in. Perhaps you have a hard time believing what others see in you because you know that you aren't always your true self. You put your best face forward, hoping that people will accept that version without uncovering the impostor you feel you are inside. As we discuss *Authenticity*, we will practice how to stay in line with your core beliefs and values while forming and maintaining important relationships. And this involves the most important relationship, which is with yourself. Make no mistake about it, authenticity involves risk, vulnerability, and letting go of anticipated shame and guilt.

Accountability is the other part of step one. Because you will need to remain accountable to (read: *compassionately and objectively honest* with) yourself. I won't lie — this is *absolutely possible,* but it takes some work. You will feel the urge to rationalize and reason that your self-assessment is *crushingly, brutally honest.* You will indulge your previous behavior of negative self-assessment, convinced that others have been fooled or misled by your public persona. And while it's likely true that some of the time you are correct, it's also true that you generally aren't as accurate (or as forgiving) of yourself as is warranted.

In step one, you will begin to form a new vision of who you are and where your internal and external behavior can start to move into greater alignment.

W—Worthiness, Wholeheartedness, Willingness

In so many ways, *Worthiness* is at the heart of the AWESOME process. However, your prior assessment of worthiness, especially when based on the achievement of external milestones, isn't the measure we will use. *Worthiness* is already yours, just as you are. You won't actually be increasing your worthiness as a human being — you will start to recognize that you are already there. *Worthiness* is not a standard of what you do, and it's not a bar that you are striving to meet. *Worthiness is inherent in who you are*. I love this statement from *Daring Greatly* (Brené Brown): "Yes, I am imperfect and vulnerable and sometimes afraid, but that doesn't change the truth that I am worthy of love and belonging." Exactly. Or as Tara Brach (*Radical Acceptance*) says, "On this sacred path of Radical Acceptance, rather than striving for perfection, we discover how to love ourselves into wholeness."

We begin to put our sense of *Worthiness* into play when we start living in a *Wholehearted* fashion. *Wholehearted* living is about engaging in our lives from a place of *Worthiness*. It means cultivating the courage, compassion, and connection to wake up in the morning and think, "No matter what gets done and how much is left undone, I am enough." (Brené Brown, *Daring Greatly*). In this chapter, we will learn ways to approach our life from a *Wholehearted* perspective. We will cover our tendency to wither and shrink, and we will practice how we can be our whole self. This is when we begin to put the pedal to the metal and surge forward. This is when we hold, screaming, onto the safety bar on the roller-coaster ride but keep breathing our way through until the end, emerging shaking yet victorious. (If you can't guess, I find roller-coaster rides terrifying. Perhaps you love them. If so, imagine surfing the big cresting wave off the shore in Hawaii, or flying excruciatingly fast down the slope when you first learned to ski and weren't quite sure how to stop. You get the idea here—the images that prompt fear, anxiety, and a sense of "Why did I ever even think about doing this?")

E—Engaging, Connecting

Step three in the AWESOME process takes you to the place of relationships. As you are practicing *Awareness*, *Authenticity*, accepting *Worthiness*, and living *Wholehearted*, you are doing it in the company of others. We will look at the ways in which you allow yourself to connect with other people, and the ways in which you hide in plain sight. We will consider who you tend to form relationships with, and the way this moves you forward or holds you back.

There's a saying that "you are the reflection of the five people you spend the most time with," and we will use this lens to up-level your internal assessment. This does not mean that you will need to ditch your current loved ones, friends, colleagues, and associates (although some of that may happen). When you allow yourself to shine and to #BeAWESOME, sometimes this results in discomfort in others. Not because you are conceited, or acting *better* than others, but because sometimes when people are struggling with their own process of self-acceptance and *Worthiness*, they shy away from those who are living in a *Wholehearted* fashion. As discussed in *Own Best Friend*, this is when it's *not about you*. We will look at how you can discern what is *your stuff* from what rightly belongs to someone else, and put that into loving practice. On the other hand, you may find that you are developing even closer, more rewarding relationships with the people who are already in your life. And that's fabulous!

S—Spirituality, Seeing

An essential component of being *awesome* is the sense of connection to what is greater than ourselves. This comes through allowing ourselves the chance to develop a practice of spirituality. While many think "religion" when spirituality is mentioned, that's not our specific focus. We will consider how to create or enhance our spiritual selves. And we will look at this from the perspective of service to others. There's a lot of research that supports the beneficial effects of altruism and giving, as well as solid evidence of the increase in happiness and contentment when we help others.

O—Openness, Forgiveness

Now we're getting into some super powerful places. This chapter will address how we can become more open to experience without diving back into fear, anxiety, or concern about failure. We will institute the practice of embracing our circumstances and using them to learn and grow, even when it seems unlikely or dismal.

Forgiveness, especially self-forgiveness, will be the path we follow to incorporating openness into our life. Using the four-fold path of forgiveness, courtesy of Archbishop Desmond Tutu, we will practice self-forgiveness and allow a more dispassionate view of ourselves to emerge. Not as revisionist history, but as a means of accepting that as human beings, we make mistakes. Holding onto resentment and anger, especially in relation to ourselves, keeps us living small and shallow. It holds us back from the expansion of the soul that is necessary to live our lives #AWESOME. And it's way past time to let go of the negative ties that bind us to our past behavior. As psychologist and author Rick Hanson reminds us, "Only we humans worry about the future, regret the past, and blame ourselves for the present" (*Buddha's Brain*). This doesn't mean that we will be constructing a sanitized version of our lives, but that we will allow our former choices and behavior to instruct us, rather than define us.

M—Mindfulness, Motivation

Finally, we will return to the idea of *Motivation* — the concept that we started to deconstruct in chapter one. This time we will develop a means of staying *Motivated* that is self-perpetuating and allows us to keep moving forward even when we don't feel like it.

We will use the practice of *Mindfulness* to guide and shape our *Motivation*. *Mindfulness* is about living in the present moment, rather than worrying about the past or the future. As defined by Jon Kabat-Zinn, "Mindfulness is awareness that arises through paying attention, on purpose, in the present moment, non-judgmentally." This does not mean that we won't plan or review our actions. It does mean that, through forgiveness and wholehearted, authentic living, we will value where we are *right now*, maximizing the potential of our life.

E—Energy

This is the final step, and it's amazing! For every time you have ever said, "It won't work," "It can't happen," or "I don't know how" — this is the answer. You will access the phenomenal power of our energetic world and master manifestation of your innermost desires. Really.

Having created the steadfast and enduring foundation of *Worthiness*, accessing *Openness* to experience and *Forgiveness* for not being perfect (and remembering that there is no such thing as perfect anyway!), you will put all the elements of AWESOME together in this step. This is the part where your dreams become reality, and your inner and outer selves are, not only aligned, but also flying high. And this is where you will learn to ride the drafts, as do the eagles, soaring to the tops of mountains and creating a life you have not yet begun to imagine.

In the next chapter, you will start the AWESOME process, learning how to increase self-awareness without judgment, how to utilize accountability from the standpoint of neutrality, and how to begin to allow your authentic self to emerge. Let's get started!

Chapter 4

Awareness, Authenticity, Accountability

It's the little imperfections
that make them unique.
—Old Dominion,
"Stars in the City"

Want to know something funny? When I started to write this chapter, I felt completely blocked. I knew what I wanted to share with you—the parts of being AWESOME that require *Awareness, Authenticity*, and *Accountability*. I gave you the overview of this in the previous chapter, and from the beginning, this has been the concept that underlies the whole process. Furthermore, I'm the one writing about the ideas that I know *work* for getting to the place of living and being #AWESOME.

So, what's the problem? Why the block? And not just

a block—I can't even tell you all the ways in which I procrastinated starting this chapter. (Good news—I'm caught up on every other minor task that I could possibly need to address. Bad news—I did it all while knowing I was procrastinating. The good news/bad news of *Awareness*: You know what you're doing as you do it. And sometimes you stay on the wrong path, even when you're fully aware that's what's happening.)

Even though I was aware that I was holding off on the writing, I wasn't clear on the *why*. In true semi-reformed, type-A, overachiever fashion, I began to consider all the possible reasons. I'm not going to list them, because none of them were true. But after wallowing in the muck of what I eventually realized was self-doubt, I came up for air. I took a breath, settled into myself, and thought about what it means to be authentic. I wrote down this sentence: "Being true to ourselves and measuring our self-worth by who we are, and how we live, rather than what we do." Yup. That's when it hit me. I was feeling scared, worried that what I was going to write wasn't *good enough*: it wouldn't be motivating, inspiring, or clear enough to pave the way for others to understand and apply in their own lives. Seriously? I was gathering *inauthenticity* around me like a cloak, shielding the true *me* from the anticipated, potential reactions of readers. Readers that won't even exist if the writing isn't done. Ugh. *This* is exactly why being awesome is a lifelong practice, a way of approaching life and circumstances that is *simple, not easy*. Because it is very easy to slip off track and into old patterns. Patterns that are sneaky in the way they present themselves, clothed like the big bad wolf in grandmother's cloak. And like the wolf, these are patterns that will eat us up if we don't keep coming back to the place of courageous vulnerability, which is being honest with ourselves.

I asked one of the women I interviewed what gets in the way of her being AWESOME and she said, "When things are not perfectly aligned, I feel like a failure." What did you think when you read that? Did you have a moment of significant empathy with her position? Or perhaps, did your heart seize up a little bit, feeling compassion for the extraordinary standard she has set for herself? Have you had a similar experience of seeing the world in an all-or-nothing kind of way, where the only options are "complete success" or "failure"? Clearly, I have had that experience (as evidenced by my difficulty in writing this chapter!). As I reviewed her quote, I was struck by how harsh she was to herself and how virtually impossible her expectations (I didn't get the sense that she was looking at failure as a growth opportunity — more like an indictment). And my thoughts immediately went to the ways in which we so often avoid challenges, opportunities, situations where we *might* feel like a failure — avoid them without even trying, so there's no actual evidence of whether we *would* succeed.

Why do we want to practice *Awareness* and *Authenticity*? In short, because when we develop awareness of our emotional state and allow ourselves to respond authentically (being true to what really matters to us), we have an amazing feeling of freedom. We are no longer expending energy in hiding and covering up, or trying to be something or someone other than we are. And this is essential for getting to the place of living unfettered by guilt or shame. When you incorporate *Awareness* and *Authenticity* into your life, you can celebrate both your strengths and your weaknesses. You can embrace a deep knowing of who you are and begin living from that awareness And you know that the one person you are ultimately accountable to is yourself. No one else can live your life, and the responsibility for who and how you are is yours.

Although this can seem daunting, in fact it is phenomenally freeing. Because no matter what anyone else thinks, says, feels, or does, your choices are up to you.

Cultivating Awareness

"The most fundamental aggression to ourselves, the most fundamental harm we can do to ourselves, is to remain ignorant by not having the courage and the respect to look at ourselves honestly and gently" (Pema Chödrön, *When Things Fall Apart: Heart Advice for Difficult Times*).

A few minutes ago, I walked outside to check on the weather (I'm writing this at a hotel in the midst of a blizzard), and I heard a man talking on the phone. It appeared he was talking to someone about getting schoolwork done, and he was very agitated. He was using strong language (including a lot of obscenities), with the central message that the other person wasn't meeting expectations. As I listened, I imagined being the person he was talking to, and how I would feel. Immediately, I felt small, incompetent, powerless. I only heard a snippet of the conversation, as I had verified that the snow was still falling, the roads were still not plowed, and it was time to end my break and get back to writing. I can't tell you what happened next for the man on the phone, or whomever he was talking to, but I can report what happened to me.

As I sat back down to write, I hesitated. Glanced at my notes and began to wonder if I was on the right track, or if I should do some more research. Oh boy. Not this again! Luckily, having just practiced *Awareness* and *Authenticity* in removing my earlier block, I was attuned to what was happening. Just hearing someone else (a stranger) had impacted my thought process. How does this happen? Thankfully, we are beginning to understand the processes of the brain through neuroscience. And even more fortuitously, I had already planned to share this explanatory quotation from Dr. Daniel Siegel with you: "One of the key practical lessons of modern neuroscience is that the power to direct our attention has within it the power to shape our brain's firing patterns, as well as the power to shape the architecture of the brain itself…. Our state of mind can turn even neutral comments into fighting words, distorting what we hear to fit what we fear" (*Mindsight: The New Science of Personal Transformation*).

Once our brain has developed a firing pattern of bringing up feelings of fear, smallness, or *less than*, we are more likely to interpret what goes on around us from that framework. And I am using this example. not just because it's current (literally, occurring as I write), but because it illustrates the subtle way in which we are susceptible to the opinions and behaviors of others. As I've mentioned, I'm the only one who is responsible for my thoughts, feelings, and actions. But that means I also need to notice when my thoughts, feelings, or actions are being triggered by an outside influence, and then assess the inner truth of what's really going on for me. While I felt compassion for the unknown person on the other end of the phone call I overheard (it's never good to be the recipient of angry obscenities), this was not about me. And it's my responsibility to notice when I am choosing to internally respond to someone else's behavior (making it about me when it's not). Frankly, it's work enough to manage your own thoughts, feelings, and actions — there's no need to take on extra baggage coming from someone else! As we understand from Dr. Siegel, "Inviting our thoughts and feelings into awareness allows us to learn from them rather than be driven by them." And so, noticing what I was feeling, increasing my awareness of my internal state, allowed me to differentiate between the link that had been triggered (feeling incompetent and powerlessness), and the reality of the situation.

Margaret, one of the women I've coached, shared that for her, to #BeAWESOME was about learning to "have a positive attitude, not be guarded, be willing to take risks, and tolerate vulnerability." I've known Margaret for many years, and she was my initial inspiration for this chapter. When I met her, I was impressed by Margaret's strength of character, her fearless attitude and determination, and her willingness to speak up and voice her opinion. Initially, I had no idea of the discrepancy between her internal perspective and how she came across in the world. I knew others shared my perception of Margaret, especially the sense of her as fearless and willing to take risks.

As Margaret and I got to know each other, I discovered the ways in which her feelings shaped her behavior. Vulnerability was anathema to her—and consequently Margaret worked hard to develop a persona of strength. While this shielded her from certain experiences, it also made it enormously difficult for Margaret to let down her guard and trust others. As a result, she had a hard time establishing deeper relationships and was often very lonely. Having been hurt on multiple occasions in her life, she had fallen into the habit of keeping people at a distance to avoid further pain. Margaret was also prone to assuming a negative outcome (which was effective in maintaining her low-risk position of avoiding vulnerability and potential hurt). And this had been going on for so long, Margaret had difficulty discerning truth from perception. Because her biggest fear, underneath everything, was that she was unlovable. That her prior experiences of being hurt were simply an accurate reflection of her lack of worth. So, the idea of showing her *true self* to someone was terrifying and held the potential for validating her worst fears.

Margaret and I started with *Awareness*. I have included our primary exercise below. She was skeptical at first, mostly because she was concerned about feeling overwhelmed by negativity and self-loathing during the exercise. As I reminded Margaret (and please, apply this to yourself), this is an exercise in information-gathering. It is not forming judgments about yourself. This is not how you determine if you are *good, bad,* or *enough*. In fact, I can give you the answer to that right now—you ARE good, AND enough. Just for being you. You are a person of worth, by virtue of existence. In this step, you are developing *Awareness* of your internal processes. You are getting data that will help you understand and map both your current position, and where you want to go.

Exercise—Try This:

Awareness comes from paying attention to what we are feeling (emotionally and physically), and then being open to the underlying messages we are giving ourselves. We also need to remember that the messages may not be the truth, and so we need to practice objectivity in seeing and accepting our fears and doubts for what they are.

How do you practice *Awareness*? Start by planning some alone time. Fifteen minutes is a great minimum guideline (you can certainly do this for a longer period—as always, go with what works best for YOU). The goal of your alone time is to allow yourself to pay attention and notice what is going on inside you. And to do this *without judgment*. It should be no surprise that this is not as easy as it sounds. Daniel Siegel (author of *The Developing Mind: How Relationships and the Brain Interact to Shape Who We Are*) reminds us that "each of us needs periods in which our minds can focus inwardly. Solitude is an essential experience for the mind to organize its own processes and create an internal state of resonance. In such a state, the self is able to alter its constraints by directly reducing the input from interactions with others."

You can use your 15 minutes to meditate, to journal, or to simply sit/lie down and let your awareness wander. The specific method isn't the important part. What does matter is to pay attention and notice. It may help to view your noticing as an observer of yourself, as if you were the technician in an experiment who is simply recording what the *subject* is experiencing. At the end of your 15 minutes of observation, make a few notes of what you noticed, including specific sensations, as well as general themes (I use a bullet-point list for this—it doesn't need to be elaborate by any means!)

Then, imagine what information this would tell you about the person who created the list. Again, if you were the experimenter, what are you learning about your *subject*? Do their thoughts and feelings center around negativity or pain? Did they include themes of being *not good enough* or themes of *happiness and confidence*? The key to this exercise is gathering information about what you experience and then looking at it from a neutral perspective.

Utilize this practice over time (maybe even keeping a journal of all your observations in one place) so you can generate some hypotheses about what comes up the most, or with the greatest intensity. There is no right answer to this exercise. There's not even a good or bad answer. It's just information. Increasing *Awareness* starts by developing the lay of the land. As you move into *Authenticity*, you will be determining whether the map you've detailed reflects how you want to feel—or whether you need to make some adjustments in the landscape.

Cultivating Authenticity

One of my favorite quotes comes from Brené Brown, in *Daring Greatly:* "Courage starts with showing up and letting ourselves be seen." As eloquent as her words are, the strongest echo is the ring of truth. Much of the time it's not easy, or comfortable, to be *seen*. One of the women I interviewed discussed her experience of *Authenticity* as "uncomfortable, scary because I'm out of the box, but becoming 'more' of who I am." What a wonderful idea — moving out of the box we create on order to fit in or be accepted. How often have you not said something or not

Achievement	Friendships	Physical challenge
Advancement	Growth	Pleasure
Adventure	Health	Power/authority
Affection	Helping others	Privacy
Arts	Helping society	Public service
Challenging work	Honesty	Purity
Change/variety	Independence	Quality of work
Close relationships	Influencing others	Quality relationships
Community	Inner harmony	Recognition
Competence	Integrity	Religion
Competition	Intellectual status	Reputation
Cooperation	Involvement	Responsibility
Creativity	Job tranquility	Security
Decisiveness	Knowledge	Self-Respect
Democracy	Leadership	Serenity
Economic security	Location	Sophistication
Effectiveness	Loyalty	Spirituality
Efficiency	Market position	Stability
Ethical practice	Meaningful work	Status
Excellence	Merit	Supervising others
Excitement	Money	Truth
Fame	Nature	Wealth
Family	Openness	Wisdom
Financial gain	Order	Work with others
Freedom	Personal development	Working alone

taken an action because you were worried about how it would be perceived? For most of us, myself included, this happens more often than we'd like to admit.

If you've read my first book, *Own Best Friend: Eight Steps to a Life of Purpose, Passion, and Ease,* then you may remember the story of my yellow car. If you haven't read it yet, or don't remember, here is a short recap. For years (seriously, 18 years!), I wanted a yellow car. While this wasn't the focus of my life, it was something I wanted, but didn't act on. Why not? Because I was afraid of what other people would think. And that's the only reason. Even as I write this, I'm shaking my head at myself and wondering what held me back. I *know* it was fear, but I'm still astonished at the degree to which *potential* worry about *other people's opinions* held me back. I wasn't contemplating an action that would impact anyone else. It wasn't even a blip on anyone else's radar screen. But when I considered taking action, I would feel flooded with fear. And it was fear that was based in potential shame. How? I was afraid that people would think I wanted to call attention to myself (which brought up the sense of shame, and not being *good enough*). I was afraid that people would think I was frivolous (same reasoning). At one point, I even recognized that I was afraid others would think less of me (I don't have an answer as to why I thought that—because logically, I knew that no one cared. It's just not a big deal).

Somehow, the idea of standing out was just too scary. And the yellow car was only one example of the ways in which I held back from being seen. I was active in the things I knew I could do well, or competently. But I wasn't a big risk-taker, especially if I had doubts about my potential performance. Those were opportunities that I passed by, masked by the reasoning that I didn't have time, or wasn't really interested. Sometimes, I even told myself that I was just being practical, since expending energy on a challenge with a low probability of success was not very sensible. Here's an example: I was a licensed, practicing clinical psychologist for 15 years before I attempted to submit a presentation proposal to my professional association (the American Psychological Association). And it was another three years after that before I wrote my first article for publication—anywhere! To put this into context, the last time I had written an article for possible publication was in high school, 35 years earlier. That's a lot of time to not even attempt to do something I enjoy (writing). That's not to say that I would have been prolific in the intervening 35 years, but given that I have written two books and about 25 articles in three years, it's probably safe to say I would have written *something*. And the only thing holding me back was fear.

How do we start to be *Authentic*? As a process, we use *Awareness* (looking within ourselves and telling ourselves the whole truth, in an objective manner). And by integrating the knowledge we've gained from *Awareness*, we allow ourselves to be vulnerable. We are willing to admit and own our true thoughts, feelings, desires, insecurities, passions, embarrassments, dreams, and imperfections. As we become more confident in own skin, we start to share this with others. We begin to be seen, just as who we are, without the armor we have been wearing in hopes of shaping others' perceptions of us.

Being *Authentic* means being true to your nature and pursuing the life and dreams that matter to you. It is about getting in touch with the values, concepts, and ideas that light your internal fire and putting them into practice, no matter what someone else thinks. It is about having faith that you are deserving, worthy, and that you matter. It is about coming to the realization that "what you are looking for is already there, not outside of you. You are already what you want to become. You are wonderful just like that. Don't try to be something else, someone else" (Thich Nhat Hanh, *Dharma Talk*).

Acting in an authentic manner is different for each of us. What is similar is that it requires not only the knowledge of what you are doing (*Awareness*), but also a commitment to putting your findings into action. This is how you begin to challenge yourself, by stepping out of your comfort zone. If you are the type of person who always says "yes," try saying no when you are stretched too thin, even if it feels difficult (and I promise, it will feel difficult to do this!). If you are prone to saying "no," then your challenge is to find the opportunities to say yes, even though it's scary (and it's likely to be scary because you risk not doing it well). At times, you will encounter the dilemma of whether you are saying yes to avoid something else, or yes out of obligation. The way you solve this dilemma of determining authentic action is to go back to your core values and investigate what you are feeling, what you want, and what is truly in alignment with being authentically you.

Exercise—Try This:

Knowing our core values is essential to living in an authentic manner. I'm certain that you are already aware of some of your values, but there may be others that you are practicing that are not in accord with who you want to be. For this exercise, look at the list of values and identify

  a) which five or six best reflect your life *as it is*
  b) which five or six best reflect the *person/life you most want* to live
  c) what actions and choices you could pursue that would allow you to *live more from the list you made in step b, above*

Choices and Actions—Finding Your Way

What does it take to go from 18 years of not doing something, to buying the car? Or beginning to write after 35 years of not writing? Through *Awareness* and *Authenticity*, I was able to develop insight into why it happened (first acknowledging that I had made choices of non-action, and then the understanding of the associated feelings and fears). The next step is the *how* of changing. It's all well and good to have insight, but if nothing changes, then you're still in the same position (and maybe feeling worse, since now you can't pretend you don't know what's going on).

There is no standard timeline for this. Sometimes the *how* of change comes close on the heels of the *why*, and other times they are very far apart. From the beginning, I knew why I hadn't bought the yellow car, and it still took 18 years to turn that around. I like to think that I was working on creating new, positive neural networks during those years, which eventually resulted in the outward manifestation of the new car. However, my wish for you is to take action *much* sooner than I did! On the other hand, the yellow car was quickly followed by a rapid increase in writing, and other activities that I used to avoid. In some ways, it was like removing a blockage from a stream, resulting in a fast-flowing river of change. In the next chapter, **W — Willingness, Worthiness, Wholehearted**, we will talk about getting the *how* into gear, and the common obstacles you will definitely encounter along the way.

Chapter 5

Willingness, Worthiness, Wholeheartedness

In order to make any permanent changes,
you have to be willing. Willing to see
things differently. Willing to experience
new ideas. Willing to listen to the people
who cheered you on rather than ones who
echoed your fears.
— **Rhonda Britten**

Willingness

Margaret, in her outward assurance and inward doubt, needed to prepare for the challenge of vulnerability. To do that, she had to welcome the experience of potentially feeling hurt, upset, disappointed, and angry. This is *Willingness* — the knowing that something may be (and likely will be) uncomfortable and deciding to experience whatever comes. It's hard to do this, especially if you're out of practice, because you've been an expert at avoiding this potential for years. Unfortunately, you can't get to the things you want (connection, love, happiness, joy) without the risk of getting hurt. It's just not possible. And realistically, you can't hold off until you're certain that there will be a positive outcome. Because that's just doing more of the same.

When you are utilizing *Willingness*, you are putting yourself directly in the path of oncoming traffic. And you don't know whether a truck will come hurtling toward you and send you flying over the guardrail, or whether a car will stop and offer you a comfortable, air-conditioned ride. You are taking a chance. And make no mistake, some of the time it won't work the way you hoped. You will absolutely encounter accidents, near-misses, and some unforeseen spectacular rides. But the only path to what you want more of is to take the chance. Of course, this doesn't mean taking blind and impulsive actions. I'm not advocating for stepping into a situation that you would caution others to avoid. If it's clear that anyone would encounter a negative outcome (and it's not just a projection of your own self-doubt), then it's not a good idea. This is about using the knowledge from your *Awareness* and *Authenticity* work to take a chance, where previously you would have held back.

One of my favorite authors is Pema Chodron. She shares her wisdom on living an authentic life in such an open, understandable manner. I usually listen to her audiobooks and find myself nodding and smiling throughout. The other day, I pushed pause after hearing this:

"The only reason we don't open our hearts and minds to other people is that they trigger confusion in us that we don't feel brave enough or sane enough to deal with. To the degree that we look clearly and compassionately at ourselves, we feel confident and fearless about looking into someone else's eyes." Exactly. This is the process of how we hold back out of fear (and what we need to do to move past the immobility). We experience feelings (or the earliest whisper of a feeling) and then extrapolate forward into the expected certainty of the feared outcome. Rather than exploring what might occur and creating an opening for change, we doggedly dig in, determined to hold the course. Using the rationale of "the devil you know is better than the devil you don't," we hold firm in our position. We don't take the risk, and so we miss the opportunity. More than that, we are creating an entire neural network that will continue to reinforce our fear and avoidance.

The most exciting concept (to my mind) of recent neuroscience research is the concept of neuroplasticity — that we can (and do) create and strengthen neural pathways all throughout our life. Another way to understand this is that we get more of whatever we pay attention to, whether it's good or bad. Neuroplasticity isn't biased. The phrase "fire together, wire together" is not preferentially geared toward what helps us, or what gets in our way. Bottom line, what we repeat, we strengthen. So as you continue the pattern of responding to vulnerability by focusing on the potential fear of being hurt, you are creating a stronger sense of *perceived* reality that this will happen. The key word in that sentence is *perceived*. You aren't collecting data and assessing the actual likelihood of being hurt. Worse, if you maintain the belief that you will get hurt, and *pretend* to take a chance, you are much more likely to see your fears actualized. We know from studies in neuroplasticity that our brain is more likely to recall an event we have determined as "meaningful." But meaningful depends on how we have interpreted the event — it's not a neutral reflection of the actual event. Instead, we can use the advice of Eckhart Tolle: "Rather than being your thoughts and emotions, be the awareness be-hind them." Willingness is about recognizing that there is risk of both hurt and joy, maintaining honest self-aware-ness and approaching vulnerability head on. Literally, be-ing *willing*: (Merriam-Webster — "done, borne, or accepted by choice or without reluctance"). Considering the idea of success *at least* as likely as not.

Worthiness

"We can judge and blame others or ourselves... Peace comes from an honorable and open heart accept-ing what is true. Do we want to remain stuck? Or to release the fearful sense of self and rest kindly where we are?" (Jack Kornfield, *The Art of Forgiveness, Loving Kindness and Peace.*) This is the essence of *Worthiness* — releasing the fearful sense of self. When you experience embarrassment, irritation, resentment, anger, jealousy, or disappointment, you are being given a signpost that leads exactly to the heart of the matter: the place where you are stuck. Each of these feelings is a red flag, alerting you to the opportunity to practice self-compassion. Of course, what we often do instead is treat this as evidence we are *not enough,* and then re-double our efforts to push those feelings away or avoid whatever we believe trig-gered the feelings.

Do you remember the last time that you felt *good enough*? While I hope this is how you feel most of the time, I suspect that's not true. What I've learned from my 25-plus years of working with people is the univer-sal, overwhelming, high-frequency occurrence of feeling *not good enough.* Adults, teens, and children, regardless of gender, race, sexuality, economic circumstance, intelli-gence, or any other metric, seem to share this in common. If I step back from individual particulars and look at the underlying theme that connects them all, it is the sense of *not good enough*. I've put this in italics, because it's not an accurate statement of truth, but rather a self-determination based on little (if any) evidence. And it's generally connected to external standards, rather than internal values. Here's an example.

I recently tried karaoke for the first time. Only the strong-arm encouragement of several very close friends, and my personal commitment to taking risks and facing my fears, enabled this to occur. Years ago (many, many years ago), I participated in glee club and choir. Even in elementary school, I was aware that singing was not going to be my lifetime career. But at that age (when most children are yelling—or whispering—rather than singing), it wasn't an issue. I was having fun, I enjoyed the activity, and I participated. By the time I reached junior high school (or what is now known as middle school), my singing ability was considerably more in question. As in, I was significantly off-key no matter if I was trying for: bass, alto, or soprano. I could tell, and if there was any doubt, the feedback from others made it clear. It was kindly suggested that my talents lay elsewhere, so I no longer participated in either glee club or choir. If that was the end of the story, it wouldn't really matter. But for me, the idea that I was *not good enough* regarding singing took root and, like a hardy weed, began to grow.

Soon, I was no longer singing along with holiday songs. When it came to "Happy Birthday," I mouthed the words and let others sing. I wouldn't sing in the car if anyone else was there (although when alone, I turned up the volume and sang my favorite song out loud). And I never, ever attended a karaoke night. My reasoning? "I'm just not into that." Ha! The truth? I was so caught up in feeling not good enough that I was terrified someone would suggest I sing. A nightmare to me would be publicly exposing my deficiency. Without belaboring the point, you can imagine the degree to which I endorsed the belief of not good enough.

What I did not do—ever—was challenge the standard that I was using. Because, really? Not good enough for what? Professional singing was never a part of the plan, so was it true that I wasn't good enough to wish someone happy birthday? Even as I write that, it seems ridiculous. Because singing happy birthday is to celebrate and acknowledge *someone else*. It has nothing to do with being good enough or not good enough. Fear, self-doubt, and a lack of self-compassion (and *Awareness*) ruled the day. I did not sing. And truthfully, I was so skillful at avoiding the issue, it didn't really come up.

As it happened, the two dear friends I mentioned were aware of my internal assessment. I had shared my fears as part of a late-night conversation, an incidental remark in response to one of my friends expressed astonishment at my karaoke naiveté. I didn't even take notice at the time, so strong and familiar was my belief that I don't sing. Can you guess where this story is leading? Naturally, the very next night after my unintended disclosure, we were part of a group that was doing karaoke. A group of about 15 were gathered together for a celebration, and karaoke was a favorite pastime of the hostess. I didn't even flinch, just enjoyed the performances of my friends and colleagues, and smiled along with the headshake that declined participation. Until my two friends pulled me aside, and told me they expected me to join in. I was flabbergasted. Seriously? I told them I didn't sing—they even knew why. I didn't want to disgrace myself, and I certainly didn't want to offend anyone with my voice (that may seem like an exaggeration to you, but to me it was a very real possibility).

And then my friends pulled out the big guns. We were

celebrating the release of our books (first one for each of us), and they questioned my commitment to *walking my talk* regarding being my #ownbestfriend. "I thought you told us you were committed to taking risks, living big, trusting in your worthiness and value in the face of self-doubt?" they asked. And I couldn't disagree, because they were accurately quoting my triumphant words of just a few hours earlier. I just hadn't imagined those words applied to *singing*. While this wasn't a life-threatening situation (like the yellow car, it was only momentous to me), I knew I had a choice. More importantly, I knew that this was a choice that would impact how I continued to move forward, or whether I re-visited being stuck. How strong was my commitment to believing in my *Worthiness*? Which was going to win—my new(er) practice of living authentically and being ok with who I was, imperfections and all? Or my long-held disinclination to *look bad* (read: feel not good enough)?

You know the answer, since I started this story telling you I tried karaoke. I got up and sang a song (facing away from the audience but singing into the microphone with passion and conviction—loudly). My face was red, my ears were burning, and internally I vacillated wildly between pride (for taking the risk) and embarrassment (I could hear myself singing). And when it was over, I had to take a few minutes for myself. I sat down outside, since my trembling legs wouldn't hold me up any longer. It took a moment before I realized that tears were streaming down my cheeks. And a few minutes more until I realized that I had demonstrated *Worthiness* to myself. I had lived up to the *only* standard that mattered—mine. My standard of not staying stuck in fear, and not letting self-doubt rule my actions. Because it was never about my singing ability. It was *always* about my *Willingness* to believe I was worthy, no matter what.

"Vulnerability is the birthplace of love, belonging, joy, courage, empathy, and creativity. It is the source of hope, empathy, accountability, and authenticity. If we want greater clarity in our purpose or deeper and more meaningful spiritual lives, vulnerability is the path" (Brené Brown, *Daring Greatly*). By taking the risk, being willing to experience vulnerability, and trusting that I was *worthy exactly I as am,* I opened the door to a deeper level of self-acceptance and self-love. When we are fully able to accept and love ourselves, we exponentially increase our capacity to love and connect with others.

Wholeheartedness

Wholeheartedness is defined as "showing or characterized by complete sincerity and commitment: (Merriam-Webster). Brené Brown, from her research on shame, (the emotion that births the idea of not good enough), defines being wholehearted as "…engaging in our lives from a place of worthiness. It means cultivating the courage, compassion, and connection to wake up in the morning and think, no matter what gets done and how much is left undone, I am enough" (*Daring Greatly*). It is the combination of *Willingness* to take action (courage in the face of vulnerability) and *Worthiness* (believing the *real* you is enough) that allows us to live wholeheartedly.

Wholehearted living is singing despite the discomfort, knowing that it's not going to be perfect (and knowing that perfect reflects a perceived external standard). It's about exposing vulnerability and living through it. And it's about realizing that my worth isn't in hitting the right notes. It's in embracing the truth of who I am and valuing myself, *as is*. I could take singing lessons. I could "improve." Or I could just start singing along when it's someone's birthday. What matters isn't which choice I make. It's knowing I have the choice. That fear and shame aren't ruling my life in the little moments. Because it's the little moments that set the stage for how we live the rest of our life.

For Margaret, living *Wholehearted* meant starting the process of sharing her inner self, knowing it was so different from what she showed the world. Margaret's journey began with saying, "I'm afraid," and continued with the expression of her concerns about being judged, found lacking, and having her true self rejected. Margaret had to do all this knowing that she could still get hurt. It was a risk, even though she was sharing this in a coaching session. She was primed to watch for the smallest hint of judgment, the tiniest confirmation that her deepest fear was becoming real, once again. She was poised to shut down and run away at the first sign of danger. Margaret used her current quotient of courage with her disclosure and didn't plan to dredge up anything more without strong evidence. Have you been in that place? Barely opening the door, with chains and locks still engaged, waiting to slam it shut—perhaps for good?

It reminds me of dipping one toe in the icy water of the pool on a hot, sunny day. You want so desperately to cool down, and the water appears inviting, offering blessed relief. But you can't stop thinking that it will be cold, too cold to actually enjoy. And you hesitate, unsure if you will regret even trying. Wouldn't it be easier to go inside? Avoid the pool and the cold water. Considering a shower instead to cool down, but realizing the muggy weather will prevent you from drying off, and will leave you ultimately hotter than before, with sticky clothes. Wavering—dive in, risking the shock (perhaps pain) of the cold, versus staying out, tolerating the heat. Weighing the cost and benefit, determined by which is the worst outcome (rather than the best). As your foot hovers over the step, you realize that what's holding you back is *fear of anticipated discomfort*. You haven't gone into the water, so you don't have accurate information about how it will be (and you're not remembering how quickly your body will adjust to the temperature). In fact, the only thing you do know is how uncomfortable you are in the present moment. Your current path isn't meeting your needs, but you're actively considering holding your course, *in case* the alternative isn't better. In truth, if you stick one toe into the water and pull it out, even if you do this several times, you will be more likely to decide that it's too cold to risk. *Wholehearted* living involves making the *commitment* to taking the plunge, and then doing it. You still have options. You can jump all in, or steadily walk down the pool stairs, gradually acclimating to the water before dunking under. But either way, you continue to move forward.

Margaret needed to practice tolerating vulnerability, beyond the point she thought she could manage. Using our pool analogy, she didn't need to dive into the deep end without knowing how to swim. But she did need to start getting wet. And the longer she hesitated, the more her fear would grow, until her assessment of the cost was no longer grounded in reality. The answer was to name her fear, and access support in addressing it and bringing it to light. Daniel Siegel refers to this brain process as "name it to tame it," referring to the calming effect of accurately labelling and owning our fear (based on cortex-involved neurotransmitter release that begins to soothe the fear-reactive limbic system). As you learned in the last chapter, this requires awareness, because we can't name a fear that we don't acknowledge. After *Awareness*, through recognizing our chosen personal values, we utilize *Willingness* to challenge our prior assessment of *Worthiness*. This is how we start to practice *Wholehearted* living.

Exercise—Try This:

Pull out your personal values list from chapter four. The one that identifies what you want to have *more of* in your life. Using this list of five to six items, create a series of potential actions or beliefs that would move you in the direction that you would like to go. Use as much creativity as possible in generating new behaviors. If you feel stuck or completely blocked, you might ask a trusted friend for ideas. Remember that what you are developing is a roadmap for experiencing and tolerating vulnerability and fear. You are likely to try to minimize any potential risk (that's perfectly ok; it's human nature). As you create your roadmap, include at least two items that seem completely out of reach (as an example, my singing karaoke would definitely have been an over-the-top, risky behavior). Keep in mind that this is for you, and as a support in your living the kind of life you most want. There's no judgment in what you find scary (or easy). And there are no right or wrong answers. There are just degrees of *Awareness*, *Willingness*, and *Authenticity*. And your *Worthiness* is already assured, no matter what you do!

For a greater challenge, pick one of your items to practice during the next week. (This is like a fitness video, where there's someone demonstrating the technique for the individual who is just starting out, and a different technique for the individual who has already started the work and mastered the initial moves). You aren't *better* if you start implementing a new behavior this week, and you aren't *worse* if you don't. This is a matter of pacing and practice. Start where you are and keep moving forward. You're on your way to creating a new neural network—one that is based in self-acceptance, rather than fear.

Chapter 6

Engagement and Commitment

You are the average of the five people
we spend the most time with.
— Jim Rohn

What did you think when you read that quote? Did you immediately start thinking about who you know? And assessing what this says about you? Did you agree? Or did it get your back up and have you saying, "That's ridiculous!"? The idea is based on the law of averages. It's a concept that has taken off within the personal development community and among entrepreneurs, holistic and spiritual practitioners, and in the world of motivational speaking.

The first time I heard this, I had a hard time defining who the five people were that I'm around the most. Did it include work? (Yes.) Spouse? (Yes.) More than that, I started to realize that I didn't spend a lot of time in the physical presence of people other than students, clients, and my husband. I have a number of good friends, but several aren't nearby. The others are generally just as busy as I am, so we don't end up spending a lot of time together (texting doesn't count). I had started to connect with some new people through online communities (a writer's group, a mental health professionals group, a coaching group), but again I was intermittent in my communication. Mostly *likes* and one- or two-word responses to posts.

The more I thought about this, the more I realized how insular my world had become. Occasional phone calls and dinners notwithstanding, I was usually helping others (i.e., working), with my husband or alone. I was struck by the contrast to my twenties and thirties, when I seemed to always be around friends. While there's certainly a natural progression over time that leads to "busyness," and there's no mistaking that I used to avoid being alone, this was still a dramatic difference. I had actively worked at developing interests, hobbies, and the skill of relaxing on my own (learning to relax was a *major* challenge — more about that when we get to chapter nine, M — *Mindfulness, Meditation, and Being Present*). But when did my world become so small? What had happened? And what did it mean that I didn't have a circle of five people?

Why is engagement so vitally important? Because *disengagement creates the belief of scarcity* – the idea that when you don't have connections with other people (meaning experiences of love, friendship, belonging), that you *won't* have those important experiences going forward. Your worldview begins to narrow, and you start imagining that it won't get better. Your mind creates a scenario in which you become increasingly isolated. Often to the point of fearing that you will end up alone for the rest of your life. (This is a fear that I have heard from almost all the people I have worked with, at some point. It may be worded differently, but the idea is the same. Being disengaged, or feeling disconnected, tends to lead to negative internal thoughts — "Something's wrong with me," or, "No one will ever like me," and these thoughts feed on themselves and grow.) But having *real* conversations increases connection, which leads to more confidence, leadership, and a richer life.

Show Me the Facts

A survey by Mental Health America found that 71 percent of people turned to friends or family in times of stress. That's not surprising. It seems natural to seek comfort and connection when you are facing a difficult situation. Harry Harlow's well-known rhesus monkey experiment from the 1950s is an example of this. Harlow (an American psychologist) separated baby rhesus monkeys from their mothers shortly after birth. He placed the baby monkeys with a surrogate made either of plain wire mesh or covered in a soft terrycloth. What Harlow observed over time was that the baby monkeys liked the cloth monkey better. More importantly, the monkeys turned to the terrycloth "mother" for cuddling and affection, *especially if something happened that was stressful or threatening*. Even though this wasn't a real mother (it was still wire mesh covered in cloth), the baby monkeys were looking for comfort when stressed. Harlow's work was important in how we understand attachment (the forming of a close bond to someone else).

John Bowlby (a British psychoanalyst) and then Mary Ainsworth (a former student of Bowlby) described and expanded our understanding of attachment through studying parent-child interactions. Ainsworth looked at infant-parent relationships and eventually developed a four-tiered framework of attachment styles (secure, anxious, avoidant, and disorganized). Attachment research has expanded into looking at adult relationships and the link between infant attachment styles and adult attachment styles. Secure attachment has multiple benefits throughout the lifespan. One study of adult attachment styles found that about 60 percent of people have a secure attachment style, characterized by *an ability to display and receive affection, caring, and acceptance* (Hazen and Shaver, 1987). In specific, adults looked for comfort and support when feeling distressed or troubled, just like the baby monkeys in Harlow's studies. Beyond that, research shows that people who demonstrate compassion to others are more open to receiving social support (and *show lower stress reactions*).

Attachment to others is the first way infants/children learn to regulate themselves and remains a primary way that we regulate throughout our lives (although we do develop the ability to self-regulate as well). Being able to modulate and manage our emotional and behavioral responses is key for happiness, productivity, and overall adaptive functioning. One recent study (Feeney and Collins, 2014) found that positive relationships are a major factor in people thriving, which they defined as "coping successfully with life's adversities and actively pursuing life opportunities for growth and development." Engaging and connecting with others has a dual value—not only are you more resistant to the negative effects of stress, but you are likely to be happier, more productive, have a greater sense of purpose, and to flourish. As far as I'm concerned, that's an awesome reason to increase your interactions and connections!

Attachment research is just one of the ways in which

we can see the value of human connection and relationships. Research tells us that increased stress leads to significant effects—physically and emotionally. Common stress symptoms include stomachache, headache, muscle tension, irritability, fatigue, aches and pains, and insomnia. In fact, research has indicated that stress is connected to your immune system—you're more likely to get a cold or other illness when stressed. Chronic stress is associated with migraine, hypertension, heart attack, ulcers, and many other effects on the body. The emotional impact of chronic stress is associated with depression, anxiety, moodiness, feeling overwhelmed, and *loneliness*.

Best stress-reducing techniques? Laughter and connecting with other people. Laughter gives us the biggest shot of dopamine (more than chocolate or good sex). Think of a time when you were upset, and then something humorous happened. Even if the difficult situation was still a concern, I bet that after laughing you felt at least a little better. Or remember a time when you started laughing and couldn't stop—you kept going until your stomach (and your cheeks) hurt from laughing so hard. It's a wonderful feeling! We get a similar boost from connecting with other people. Research shows that having a support network increases feeling of self-worth, security, and a sense of belonging—as well as helping your body and immune system stay healthy. Further, you get physical and emotional health benefits from *giving* support as well as *receiving* support (just make sure it's a two-way street, since an imbalance in support can be really draining).

The Value of Connection

The other day my friend Jenny shared her theory that most business models are male-oriented, pointing out that the standard way we introduce ourselves to each

other ("Hello, I'm Kristina. I'm a therapist") only rein-
forces the typically masculine concept that what we do
is what we *are*. As the conversation progressed, I thought
of the many times I have done *just that thing*, and how
disconnected it feels. I don't want to be defined by what I
do (and I can't come up with a short enough sentence to
describe my many passions).

Ever have one of those weeks where *every single day*,
the same theme comes up? My conversation with Jenny happened after I returned from a two-day workshop
with the amazing Chris Winfield. Chris is a super-con-
nector, dedicated to the mission of real conversations
with real people. Because "real people are . . . real people." (Love that quote!) And the day in between Chris's
magic and Jenny's wisdom, I re-connected with a friend
from college. She sent me a message, and we jumped on
the phone right away. 34 years since we had last talked,
and the time melted away. What's the point of these stories? Each interaction resulted in *new, win-win opportunities* for each of us (both regarding business and in terms
of increasing our personal circle of influence). And the
magic happened because *it was about connecting.*

The morning after seeing Jenny, I was listening to
Brené Brown's talk, *The Power of Vulnerability,* as I was
driving. Here's what she said: "... the underpinning of
scarcity is disengagement ... the absence of love and belonging always results in suffering...." Same theme, same
message. I admit—I'm a mega-fan of Brené Brown. Because she talks about real things that happen in the lives
of everyone. Shame, vulnerability, fear—none of us are
exempt (no matter how much we pretend).

How is this relevant to you? You are a real person.
And when you connect with other people in a genuine
fashion, you form relationships. I don't mean network-
ing—because all too often, that's the same old *show you*

what I want you to see model. I'm talking about actually knowing something about someone else. And being interested, because people are interesting when you see them 3D, and not as a business opportunity or a chore. The other piece of magic? When you are connecting, you step out of scarcity mode. Instead of worrying about impressing or being liked—both of which are thinly veiled concerns about not being enough—you are opening the door to abundance. You begin to realize that you do not have to be isolated or alone. You start to find new people everywhere. You stop worrying about whether your grain of sand will be noticed and start appreciating what it feels like to be part of the beach. And it feels *great*!

There is no limit to love, or connection, or opportunity. All it takes is *being you and being with* the other person.

Purpose of the Five-Person Circle—"Up-Leveling"

After determining who the five people are that you spend the most time with (or initially in my case, the one to two people), the next step is to get a read on how well, and how consistently, you contribute to each other's growth. If you're the leader of the pack, constantly challenging yourself, trying new things, and providing the inspiration, there's a piece you're missing. We reach new heights through association with those who are functioning at or above us. If you're head and shoulders above everyone else (in attitude and action), it's much harder for you to keep improving. Consider the training of budding (or professional) athletes. If golf is your passion, you want to play with and learn from people who are better golfers. The four-times-a-summer golfer takes a completely different approach to the game than the golfer who is trying to reduce their handicap from eight to five. This is true across all sports, as well as in business.

The topics for consideration over lunch among Fortune 500 CEOs differs from the conversation among brand-new, startup entrepreneurs. It's not entirely dissimilar (after all, people are people). But the answer to, "How do I grow my business?" is going to address widely varied topics between those two groups.

Beyond the basics of conversation and business connections, there is often a different approach to problem-solving, which is most noticeable in attitude. For the business owner who wants to keep expanding, a creative and can-do attitude is necessary. Maintaining momentum is easiest when we are in the position of seeing colleagues who are committed to the same kind of goals. On the other hand, when what you hear most often is someone's fear of failure or *can't-do attitude*, it's harder to keep moving forward. This is just as true when it comes to personal growth and development. When your focus is on facing fear, embracing authenticity, and living in a wholehearted manner, you will have the greatest success when you spend time with others who are equally engaged and committed. Anne's story illustrates how good intentions sometimes aren't enough.

Anne had been working at mid-level jobs for years. She wasn't satisfied and frequently felt stuck. After considerable soul searching, she identified her passion, along with a secret dream to leave her current situation and follow her passion full-time. Anne started talking with those in her five-person circle, and the reception she got was lukewarm at best. The most common themes were, "It's too risky" and a version of, "Why upset the apple cart?" Anne's circle of five was made up of wonderful people who cared about her deeply and absolutely wanted her to have happiness and success. But none of them were taking major personal risks themselves. They were caught in the cycle of *can't-do*, able to give long lists of what might go wrong and struggling to find their own momentum. As you can imagine, it didn't take long for Anne's enthusiasm to wane and her steps to falter.

Anne and I had met a few months earlier, and I had watched her personal growth skyrocket. She was exploring new activities, meeting new people, and letting go of some of the limiting beliefs she had developed years ago. Her face lit up when discussing her passion, and she literally seemed to bounce in her chair when she outlined her ideas for a new approach to her work life. But the closer she got to actualizing this dream, the more she seemed to lose steam. Her conversation started to shift from excited exploration to self-doubting and questioning. This was when we began to look more closely at her inner circle. It didn't take long for Anne to realize that her closest connections weren't in line with her future goals, and she had begun to give their opinions additional weight (over her own). After all, these were the people she was around the most (and she knew how much they cared about her).

The answer wasn't for Anne to ditch her whole support network. But it was time for her to assess whether her need for inspiration, encouragement, and a success-orientation was going to be met as things stood. Anne began to seek out people who were in a similar growth stage and develop some new relationships. She still valued her friends, but she also recognized she couldn't always be the leader (and the cheerleader) for everyone else. She needed some of her golf matches to be with more advanced golfers (figuratively speaking, since golf was absolutely *not* her passion). As Anne sought out new mentors and role models, her spark returned. The light was on, the passion was back, and she was in motion. She did not end up leaving her job, but she did reorganize her priorities to ensure she had more time to pursue her interests. As this continued, Anne noticed an increasing sense of happiness and positivity. As she put it, "I got my mojo back."

What happened with her initial group of friends? Two of the relationships became a little more distant, as neither of them felt they had as much in common as before. The other three relationships started to deepen and become richer (Anne had shared some of her insights and reflections with them). And Anne's circle of five had shifted, with the introduction of two new dynamic connections.

Exercise—Try This:

Identify the five people in your life that you spend the most time with, considering their approaches to life, challenges, and attitudes regarding your hopes and dreams. Do they *know* your hopes and dreams? What tends to be the topic of conversation?

When I did this exercise for myself the first time, I discovered that my husband and I talked about the weather a *lot*—an inordinate amount of time. What?!? I'm used to telling people what a wonderful primary relationship I have, and I had no idea how often we fell into the habit of generic conversation. There's no real reason for the weather to take a central position in our lives. We're not meteorologists, we don't work outside for a living, and weather doesn't usually have a major impact on what we do. I realized that we were cheating—relying on superficialities, rather than connecting. We talked about this, and both made a commitment to sharing more of ourselves with each other. We still talk about the weather (we live in New England, so the weather can change on a dime), but it's a sentence or two, and usually makes us laugh, paving the way to conversation that connects us instead of keeping us apart.

Bonus Exercise

Approach someone today that you don't know that well (or even a stranger) and start a conversation with them. Ask about their favorite color, and why. Or any other question that pops into your mind when you're open to really seeing and connecting to *who they are.* While you're learning about them, practice being open and sharing something about you. Using your practice of *Awareness* from chapter four, notice what this feels like, emotionally and physically in your body. Not sure how to find someone? How about in line at Starbucks, at the grocery store, or at work? This doesn't have to be a three-hour conversation. It just needs to be a moment of real connection and engagement. Do this while practicing active listening, meaning focus on *hearing* what the other person is saying, rather than thinking about how you will respond (hint: a short pause before answering is ok, so don't get caught up in planning your reply and miss the opportunity). If this feels like too much of a stretch now, keep it in mind. In chapter eight (O — *Openness and Forgiveness*) we will delve further into *Openness*, and you'll have more chances to practice. If you do try the bonus exercise, challenge yourself to see how many days in a row you can keep going. After a week, check back in with yourself and see how this practice affects your daily mood and self-confidence. And share the magic with me — because it's all about connecting!

Chapter 7

Spirituality and Seeing

*The fact that I can plant a seed and it
becomes a flower, share a bit of knowledge
and it becomes another's, smile at someone
and receive a smile in return, are to me
continual spiritual exercises.*
— **Leo Buscaglia**

The importance of spirituality for mental wellness
has been widely acknowledged in the field of
mental health and related areas. Research by the
Mental Health Foundation in the U.K. has identified several common themes among definitions of spirituality,
including:
- a sense of purpose
- a sense of connectedness — to self, others,
  nature, "God," or Other
- a quest for wholeness
- a search for hope or harmony

- a belief in a higher being or beings
- some level of transcendence; the sense there is more to life than the material or practical
- those activities that give meaning and value to people's lives

In addition, research demonstrates that a sense of spirituality is a valuable tool in coping with stress. What resonates with me in these themes is the idea of purpose, connection, and a sense of meaning. When I was in training during my doctorate (many, many decades ago), I remember a supervisor telling me that people tend to turn to spirituality during mid-life and beyond. He cited research that validated his point. As a young twenty-something, I was skeptical. I had grown up with a family-driven religious practice and moved away from anything even remotely religious after graduating from college. I was surprised (and shocked) to learn this—I thought my particular experience was unique to my circumstances, and I was still decades away (thankfully) from mid-life. I clearly remember my slightly hostile, highly questioning reaction. What was the rationale for people turning to spirituality/religious practice, especially after being immersed in the realities of day-to-day living? What I didn't yet understand was the greater meaning, and the enormously positive effects, of a sense of spirituality.

What Is Spirituality?

Martin Seligman, psychologist, author, past president of the American Psychological Association, and *father of positive psychology*, names spirituality as one of the 24 character strengths that human beings share. He defines spirituality as "… [religiousness, faith, purpose]: Having coherent beliefs about the higher purpose and meaning of the universe; knowing where one fits within the larger scheme; having beliefs about the meaning of life that shape conduct and provide comfort" (Values in Action [VIA] Character Survey). His research notes the universality of spirituality across all cultures: "Although the specific content of spiritual beliefs varies, all cultures have a concept of an ultimate, transcendent, sacred, and divine force" (Peterson and Seligman, 2004). I am fascinated by the idea that all cultures share a belief in a transcendent force. Today, it's an idea that makes sense to me, having passed well into mid-life. As I learned (and experienced) different life stages, I began to understand the way in which connecting to something larger than myself was both reassuring and exciting. Instead of being a single island in the sea of humanity, I began to consider myself as a part of the ocean. I did not solely determine the timing of the tides, but I saw myself as an active participant, contributing to the water that makes up the waves.

Why is *Spirituality* important and necessary to be a happier and healthier person? One of my coaching clients, Mary, recently told me that she sees the concept of *Spirituality* as frequently being superficially a divisive force, but at its roots, spiritual beliefs and values are often what we have most in common with others. Mary discussed her idea that underlying all the major religious frameworks are the basic themes of compassion, caring for others, community, service, etc. She went on to describe how it seems easier to accept an *us vs. them* mentality than it is to really take the time to listen and understand each other as human beings. But it is through the courage to sit with this discomfort and to push back against the culture of dichotomy (religious vs. not religious, or conservative vs. liberal) that we end up connecting with common humanity. This topic came up in our coaching as we focused on how she could increase *Engagement* and *Commitment*. Mary had been feeling isolated and alone. She wanted "more" in her life, but she was afraid of hurt and disappointment. As we developed goals for her in this arena, I thought of the life-changing realization shared by one of the women, Tami, I had interviewed for this book.

Tami is completely committed to self-actualization and self-care and is living her goal to #BeAWESOME. As a young woman, Tami had faced many challenges in her life and had consequently developed a series of beliefs and attitudes that kept her *living small*. The biggest hurdle for Tami was her feeling of being separate (and worse off) than those around her. She told me that her life changed in the moment she realized, "I am not alone." She had been at a large work-related event and had witnessed woman after woman telling the story she previously thought lived only in her heart. Tami still gets choked up when she relates how meaningful it was to experience a connection to people she knew nothing about—strangers sharing space in a large conference room, connected through the verbalization of dreams and disappointments, visions and fears.

Brené Brown's research in the areas of courage, vulnerability, empathy, and shame led to her conceptualization of spirituality centering around the idea of connection and compassion. These were the very components that so moved Tami, and that were invaluable to Mary as she worked towards embodying her best self. When Tami talked about her AWESOME, she mentioned a sense of confidence, power, strength, joy, happiness, and empathy. Tami "plays to [her] strengths" and is willing to acknowledge the many areas of success and well-being she has developed through this practice. Tami's advice to other women (that she lives every day): "True humility isn't downplaying your strengths and capacity but being honest and real—owning your talents and being comfortable with who you are." And she credits her expanded sense of spirituality as the catalyst for her growth. As you can imagine, I thought of Tami when I read this quote: "The highest spiritual practice is self-observation without judgment" (Swami Kripalu). Understanding the connection between self-love, self-compassion, and *Spirituality* created a higher level of personal understanding.

As I delved further into research on spirituality and mental wellness, I came across an article on mental health and spirituality. The article described the essential aspects of mental well-being as the "ability to take responsibility for one's own actions, flexibility, high frustration tolerance, acceptance of uncertainty, involvement in activities of social interest, courage to take risks, serenity to accept the things which we cannot change, courage to change the things which we can change, the wisdom to know the difference between the above, acceptance of handicaps, tempered self-control, harmonious relationships to self, others, including Nature and God." I was struck by the phrase, *"harmonious relationships to self, others, including Nature and God."*

While I don't believe everyone needs to agree on universal nomenclature to describe a presence or connection *greater than the self,* I immediately saw how this connected with Seligman's research, Brown's research, Mary and Tami's thoughts, and my own experience. Although we each used slightly different words, we were all talking about the same basic idea. We are not alone, and we are connected to everyone and everything else. I have felt my most spiritually connected when walking outside, either through the woods, by the ocean, or across a meadow. Seeing the majesty of mountains, the illumination of a sunrise, or the velvety dark night punctuated by starlight all evoke the same feeling in me. It is a sense of being a part of "something"—whatever that is—and sharing this with the rest of the world. Deepak Chopra captures this as he states:

"Enlightened leadership is spiritual if we understand spirituality not as some kind of religious dogma or ideology but as the domain of awareness where we experience values like truth, goodness, beauty, love and compassion, and also intuition, creativity, insight and focused attention."

Seeing and Embracing Our Sacred Self

> *And then I learned the spiritual journey*
> *had nothing to do with being nice. It*
> *was about being real, authentic. Having*
> *boundaries. Honoring my space first,*
> *others second. And in this space of self-*
> *care being nice just happened, it flowed*
> *not motivated by fear but by love.*
> **— Michelle Olak**

Brené Brown discusses spirituality in the context of *Wholehearted* living and *Worthiness*. "Not religiosity but the deeply held belief that we are inextricably connected to one another by a force greater than ourselves — a force grounded in love and compassion. For some of us that's God, for others it's nature, art, or even human soulfulness. I believe that owning our worthiness is the act of acknowledging that we are sacred. Perhaps embracing vulnerability and overcoming numbing is ultimately about the care and feeding of our spirits" (*Daring Greatly*).

Wholehearted living is essential to the AWESOME process and living your best life. As Brené Brown's research shows, to live wholeheartedly, we must acknowledge our common bonds, our shared vulnerability, and own our strengths within a greater framework of *connection*. The women I interviewed and those I coach describe this as:

- A sense of who I am in the world
- I choose my destiny, doing things outside my comfort zone

- I experience love, joy, and generosity and feel my own strength
- The fullest expression of my greatest potential
- Trusting myself and connecting to others
- Positive attitude, risk-taking, vulnerability, and not being guarded
- Leading with love, being present and aware
- Feeling joy, energized — I'm most in service to others when I'm my most real
- It's risk-taking — it's uncomfortable, scary, out of the box — and I know I'm part of something bigger than myself

Embracing *Spirituality* does not mean that you need to join a convent, a synagogue, or a monastery. Formal religious practice, paganism, yoga — it doesn't matter. What does make a difference is having a sense of belonging and *connection* to energy/presence, the seen/unseen, or the universe, however you conceptualize it. Throughout this book, we have emphasized the need for awareness, acknowledgment, and authentic expression of you. So, however this works for you, whatever definition (or lack of definition) rings true — that's what you focus on. Don't worry about whether or not anyone else has the same views. We've looked at the commonalities between the definitions of spirituality, and we reviewed the benefits of spirituality to your overall well-being (one additional note on that front — a sense of spirituality also has a significant stress-reducing effect).

"How we pay attention determines our experience. When we are in doing or controlling mode, our attention narrows and we perceive objects in the foreground — the bird, a thought, a strong feeling. In these moments we don't perceive the sky — the background of experience, the ocean of awareness" (Tara Brach, psychologist, author and well-known Buddhist mindfulness meditation teacher *True Ref-*

uge). When we open ourselves to *Awareness* of our full self (mind, body, spirit) and to awareness of the inter-connectedness of everything around us, we can see what was previously hidden. You experience this when you are willing to suspend judgment and pre-conceived perceptions and live in the present moment with an open mind.

I was listening to Jack Kornfield's audiobook *No Time Like the Present* today before writing this chapter. He told a story of a former soldier waiting in line at the supermarket, eager to make his purchases and get on with his day. Ahead of him in line was a woman with a young baby. The former soldier was irritated and frustrated at the slow-moving line, the chattiness of the woman with the baby, and the selfishness and lack of consideration he felt both customer and cashier showed for the rest of the patrons. As he finally placed his groceries on the belt, his distress peaked when the cashier reached over and picked up the baby. Clearly seeing his disgruntlement, the woman ahead of him turned and apologized. She explained that the baby was the daughter of the cashier—who had lost her husband in military service the year before. This was their brief daytime contact, as the cashier worked full-time to manage as a single mother of a young child. In that moment, everything shifted for the former soldier. No longer irritable and frustrated, he was filled with compassion and a feeling of connection to the woman, the baby, and the cashier. He recognized the limitations of his perceptions and his assessment of the situation.

Exercise—Try This:

Increase your sense of connection and *Spirituality* by trying one (or more) of these activities. Spending time in nature or appreciating beauty (art, music, natural, or man-made creations) helps decrease stress and increase feelings of connection, hope, meaning, and purpose. Engaging in breath-connected practice (yoga, meditation, tai chi, qigong) supports physical, emotional, and mental health. Reflection and contemplation are opportunities to increase your awareness of yourself and the larger community.

- Practice writing in a journal or creating an art journal, using the time for prayer or reflection
- Take a yoga class
- Listen to a guided meditation or a guided body scan (YouTube has an enormous selection of guided meditations)
- Engage in a contemplative practice through a spiritual community (church, prayer group, meditation center, etc.)
- Watch a nature-guided relaxation video or listen to nature-sound audio
- Spend five minutes outside, noticing whatever sensations you experience in your body

Chapter 8

Openness and Forgiveness

*What if you simply devoted this year
to loving yourself more?*
— Anonymous

Openness

In chapter five we discussed *Willingness*, which
centers around the idea of being ready and prepared
to take an action (we looked at this in terms of trying
a new or different action and being prepared to take a
risk). *Openness* is connected to *Willingness* but is more
clearly understood as consideration of different and
new ways of doing and thinking about things (action
and mindset). By definition, *Openness* is *acceptance of
or receptiveness to change or new ideas*. As you can imagine, this is a vitally important factor on your journey
of personal growth. If you aren't willing to try something new, or to remain objective and see what hap-

pens without predicting the ending, then your ability to make significant internal changes is going to be seriously hampered.

If you are someone who struggles with openness, you may come by your reluctance through a combination of genetics and experience. Psychologists define openness to experience as one of "The Big Five" personality traits (meaning it is one of the common personality traits, and how much openness we have can vary from a lot to very little). In this case, openness to experience refers to "the extent to which a person actively seeks and appreciates different experiences and tolerates and explores novel situations" (Pervin, 2002). People who have high openness to experience tend to be interested in learning new things and taking new actions, especially in areas that involve creativity. These are the people you would describe as creative, imaginative, and frequently adventurous. If openness to experience isn't as strong for a person, they will tend to take fewer risks, show less creativity (including in their thinking), and be more likely to follow regular routines.

Afraid this means you are stymied before even starting to challenge yourself? Not at all! There's recent research from Johns Hopkins University that indicates that you can increase your openness to experience through cognitive training. In the study, older adults were given a series of cognitive training sessions which resulted in an increase in openness that was stable for years afterwards. Since we tend to think of older adults as being more cognitively rigid (and less open), this finding has major implications for all of us. We can literally learn to become more open to new experiences. As mentioned previously, advances in neuroplasticity also show that we can create new behaviors, habits, and beliefs through creating new neural pathways—and this is a process that continues throughout our lifespan. Can't teach an old dog new tricks? Yes, you can, and there's an overwhelming amount of scientific proof. The other side of the coin is that when we are not working to increase our *Openness*, we are prone to increasing social isolation, and decreasing flexibility in our thinking.

F.E.A.R—What you stop doing is as important as what you start doing.

A specific note regarding *Openness*: It is connected to allowing yourself to be *in* the experience, to enter and remain in the moment without judgment (and without anticipating a specific outcome, especially a negative outcome). Are you familiar with the acronym F.E.A.R.? As an acronym, it stands for "False Evidence Appearing Real." When we are feeling fear, such as anticipated concern about trying a new behavior, the fear is often based on erroneous assumptions (we all know the saying about assumptions). In this type of circumstance, we are creating a belief system, a series of thoughts that lead to an anticipated outcome. But if we aren't looking at the underlying emotion driving the thoughts, and we aren't being objective about the accuracy of the beliefs, then we end up with F.E.A.R. being the cause of our fear. This is a common process and is frequently rooted in our concerns about either needing to be perfect or the idea of being not good enough. (I believe that most of what we fear, worry about, or hold back from can be boiled down to the thought of *not good enough*. This is what we discussed in detail with *Worthiness*.)

Of course, there's a solution. Decades of research in cognitive therapy has identified a workable alternative — challenge (or *dispute*) your beliefs. This is the practice of gathering evidence (from a neutral or objective standpoint) and seeing if the evidence fits the (assumed) belief. I suggest thinking of yourself as a scientist testing a hypothesis (whatever it is that has you experiencing F.E.A.R.). As a scientist, your goal is to gather data (the objective evidence that supports or disproves your initial belief).

Here's an example of looking at fear and anxiety and identifying F.E.A.R. as false. Stacey, one of my coaching clients, was stuck in the relationship desert. She hadn't been involved in a romantic relationship for quite some time, and she had concluded that she would never have a partner. Her prior relationships had involved a series of painful break-ups and disappointments. She recognized that her attitude about connecting with someone new was influenced by her history, but she was completely convinced that her conclusion was accurate. "I'm just not the kind of person who is able to have a long-term relationship. It's not going to happen," was her automatic reply. We looked at this belief from the aspect of F.E.A.R. as she was learning the AWESOME coaching process. In fact, Stacey has a significant number of long-term friendships, spanning back to childhood. We laid out the evidence from a neutral perspective: Had she ever had a long-term relationship? How often did this occur? Did her relationships end quickly 100 percent of the time? Were there any notable similarities among the men she had dated? How willing was she to take the risk of potential disappointment? Was there any other conclusion she could reach rather than *I'm not capable*?

Stacey used structured journaling to assess this issue, practicing the perspective of non-judgment and concrete data collection (meaning she had to consider all her relationships, not just the ones she identified as *failed*). She had to be objective in her assessment, instead of attaching greater weight to an experience because it was painful or didn't have the outcome she wanted. By following this process, Stacey quickly realized that she had the capacity to have long-term relationships (her friendships were a great example) and remembered romantic relationships that she grew out of that didn't involve pain or disappointment. Most importantly, Stacey realized that her belief ("I won't ever have a relationship") was completely blocking her *Openness* to meeting new people. Her belief was also preventing her from imagining a different outcome. You can imagine what happened next. Having confronted and named her concerns from a compassionate and realistic approach (she has experienced both happiness and sadness in her relationships) and having identified the false beliefs that were keeping her in the *desert*, she needed to apply *Willingness, Worthiness* and *Openness* to move forward. Once she started to view her situation from this perspective, she behaved differently. She entered social situations with the idea, "I'm going to have a nice time and meet new people," instead of, "No one here will have any interest in me." This allowed her to be more of herself — the person her long-term friends and family absolutely adored. And you know there's a happy ending. Stacey did meet someone and begin a new romantic relationship. Naturally, she still had some trepidation, but she continues to remind herself that openness to new experience is the fastest route to getting what she wants.

Tara Mohr, in her book *Playing Big: Find Your Voice, Your Mission, Your Message*, talks about the approach to risk (what we are calling *Openness*) in this way: "Playing big doesn't come from working more, pushing harder, or finding confidence. It comes from listening to the most powerful and secure part of you, not the voice of self-doubt … Attachment to praise and avoidance of criticism keeps us from doing innovative, controversial work and — more simply — from following the paths we feel called toward, whether or not those around us understand or approve." This is our goal in practicing *Openness*: to identify what we want in our lives, and to be receptive to new approaches and new outcomes.

The Stuck Places

Here are some of the most common phrases I've heard from my coaching clients and the women I interviewed for this book:

"I couldn't figure out an answer to 'What do I want?' or 'Who am I?'"

"I couldn't say what would give me pleasure."

"Where am I in all of this? I just couldn't figure it out."

"I was stuck with the question—'Who am I and what do I want?'"

"I knew I was holding myself back, but I didn't know why or what to do about it."

"We see what we want in others … and then we have difficulty in asking for help or trying it ourselves."

"As a people-pleaser, I've always worried about other people's opinions. I've ended up an over-achiever, even when it comes to being too hard on myself."

"I wanted to fit in, and I couldn't stop worrying about what other people think of me."

In order to come up with solutions to these dilemmas, you have to be willing and open to discovering and trying new things. Otherwise, you stay like the hamster on a wheel, running as fast as you can and getting nowhere, other than tired and discouraged. Author and happiness thought-leader Gretchen Rubin (*The Happiness Project*) takes the idea of *Openness* to the next step. "When I thought about why I was sometimes reluctant to push myself, I realized that it was because I was afraid of failure—but in order to have more success, I needed to be willing to accept more failure." Instead of repeating the same actions over and over (I'm remembering Einstein's definition of insanity), you need to try something new. And do this even when you can't guarantee the outcome. It helps if you take a different approach to failure—seeing it as a means of gaining more knowledge and experience, rather than as a reflection of your worth. Because you are always worthy. When something doesn't go the way you'd like, it's not because you aren't good enough as a human being. You may require more practice, additional skill, or a new approach, but it is *not about your worth.*

Exercise—Try This:

Don't give in to your fears. If you do, you won't be able to talk to your heart.
— Paulo Coelho,
author of *The Alchemist*

There's an exercise described by psychologist Peter Levine (author of *Waking the Tiger*) that is helpful in decreasing the anxious feelings that come up when you start (or even contemplate) doing something new. It's a form of self-hug. Put your right hand under your left armpit, with your thumb facing up towards the top of your shoulder. Wrap your left hand around your right bicep and squeeze gently with both hands. Notice how you feel and allow yourself to feel supported. See if there are any changes in your emotions, the sensations in your body, or your breathing. Ideally, see if you can maintain this position for a few minutes as a means of shifting your perceptions.

A second self-holding exercise is to put your left hand on your heart and your right hand on your belly (you can do this standing, sitting or lying down). Describe to yourself all of the different sensations that arise where your hands are touching your body. After a couple of minutes, switch your hands (right hand on your heart and left hand on your belly). Again, notice whatever sensations come up. Interestingly, most people find they have a preference for one side or the other, but there's no specific meaning related to left hand on your heart or right hand on your heart. Give it a try!

As you are practicing these forms of self-care, consider this quote from Gretchen Rubin: "It's about living in the moment and appreciating the smallest things. Surrounding yourself with the things that inspire you and letting go of the obsessions that want to take over your mind. It is a daily struggle sometimes and hard work, but happiness begins with your own attitude and how you look at the world" (*The Happiness Project*).

Forgiveness

Finding a way to extend forgiveness to ourselves is one of our most essential tasks. Just as others have been caught in suffering, so have we. If we look honestly at our life, we can see the sorrows and pain that have led to our own wrongdoing. In this we can finally extend forgiveness to ourselves; we can hold the pain we have caused in compassion. Without such mercy, we will live our own life in exile.

— Jack Kornfield,
Bringing Home the Dharma

In order to develop the ability for self-*Forgiveness*, you have to engage in self-compassion. Empathy and compassion are often confused. For our purposes, empathy is the ability to feel the pain and suffering of others. Compassion is the gentle caring and cognitive understanding of how someone is feeling, without taking on the feelings of the other person. Compassion is about feeling *for*, not feeling the feelings *of*, the other person. There's a lot being written these days about "being an empath" or what it means to be overly empathic. In terms of empathy, too much can be problematic. If we are in the position of becoming distressed ourselves about someone else's suffering, we are less able to support or help them. As humans, we are all wired the same. When we are experiencing a high level of distress, it interferes with our ability to access our cognitive (and emotional) internal resources. On the other hand, having compassion (understanding) allows us to connect with others and still access our best internal resources, which allows us to offer more constructive support and assistance.

Recent neuroscience research has supported the differences in empathy and compassion from a brain perspective. Tania Singer and Olga Klimecki trained groups of people in practicing empathy or compassion. Here's what was really fascinating. The empathy group described their experience as uncomfortable, while the compassion group showed more positivity and were more likely to help others than were members of the empathy group. The actual brain areas that were triggered were different—the empathy group showed activity in the parts of the brain associated with emotion, self-awareness, and pain. The compassion group showed activity in the areas of the brain associated with decision-making, learning, and reward. As I discussed in *Own Best Friend*, Kristin Neff is an excellent resource on developing self-compassion. Her psychological research has demonstrated the many benefits of learning to treat ourselves with compassion. (You can find a link to her website and her research in the Endnotes of this book.)

It's a Practice

Like so many other concepts, *Forgiveness* is a practice. This is particularly true when learning self-forgiveness. I have worked with many women who have developed the ability to forgive others, but just get stuck when it comes to themselves. (This is part of what motivated me to write *Own Best Friend*, because I believe that we all need to develop the skill of treating ourselves with compassion and care, and that definitely requires forgiveness!). *Forgiveness* is not about forgetting things that were hurtful, nor is it about dismissing the importance of whatever has occurred. However, forgiveness *is* about releasing the *ties that bind*. That includes being able to release the emotions that have you all knotted up, even against yourself.

Have you ever gotten two necklaces tangled up together? If even one of them is a small link chain, it can be a bear to untangle. The more you try to pull them apart and separate them, the tighter the knot seems to grow. Sometimes you are successful at getting most of the tangles undone, and then there's the last one. It just won't budge. You try gently shaking it, maybe ask someone else for help (because if you're like me, you've gotten frustrated that it's not *getting fixed*). Maybe you even pull out a safety pin and laboriously attempt to separate minuscule links without breaking the whole necklace, while your temper frays and you begin to sweat. You're not able to wear the necklace until it's unknotted, and it can easily feel like it's just too much work. This is one of the images I share with my coaching clients when we are looking at self-forgiveness. Their thoughts and emotions are twisted up, and no amount of working at it seems to make a difference—freedom from the snarl just doesn't seem possible.

What's getting in the way of solving this problem? The emotional reaction. The longer you are poking and prodding at the necklace, chances are the more your emotions are getting involved. Frustration (or sadness or feeling incompetent) has an impact on your physical reactions. As emotional tension mounts, so does physical tension. If your emotions are involved, you are actually less likely to undo the knot. Walking away, taking a few deep breaths, and then returning to it when you are calm increases your chance of success (both through your physical ability and your cognitive ability to think of creative solutions). How is this connected to self-forgiveness? When we are focused on what we have done *wrong*, we are facing the past (a situation we can no longer directly impact, because it's over). When we are focused on what might happen, we are facing the future (which we can't impact because it hasn't happened yet). What we need to do is to *stay in the present*. Avoid getting caught up in self-denigration or worry (emotions that hamper our freedom). As we stay in the present, and step away from the emotional reactions of past and future, we can determine what we can *learn* from the situation. Integrating the knowledge of what we learn into our choices going forward and practicing self-compassion loosen the knot. We are able to return to the situation and calmly untangle, using our best decision-making process.

Kim really struggled with *Forgiveness*. Worst of all, she thought she was the only one. She would look at the posts of her friends on Facebook and lament, "I look at other women and it seems seamless. I must be doing something wrong because I can't balance family, work, life, and find a place for me." Kim regretted some of the choices she had made in her life and felt like she was still paying the price.

She carried a deep belief that she "deserved" to struggle (although she didn't initially describe it that way). When I broached the idea of self-compassion and self-forgiveness, Kim immediately shook her head no. She couldn't envision how that would be possible, and believed she had to keep the past active in her mind so she wouldn't forget and make the same mistakes again.

Utilizing the AWESOME process, Kim began to make strides in the areas of *Awareness*, *Authenticity*, and *Engagement*. But *Worthiness* wasn't working because *Forgiveness* had stalled the process. This is a great example of the ways in which the AWESOME steps are intertwined. For most of us, these are interlocking concepts that we practice in an ongoing manner. Moving forward a little in one direction, with a sidestep to focus on another area. Sort of like tacking into the wind—if you've ever sailed (or watched) someone sailing in a strong wind, you know how many zigs and zags there are to get from point A to point B. And then sometimes the wind shifts, and it's a smooth, straight path.

For Kim, understanding the words of Maya Angelou was transformative: "Forgive yourself for not knowing what you didn't know before you learned it." Kim was able to see that she was judging herself from her current knowledge perspective, not based on what she knew then. Of course, the judging part also needed to be released. But using the scientist-exploring-a-hypothesis method, Kim became clear that she had made the best decisions she could, based on what she knew and who she was at the time.

Exercise—Try This:

Jack Kornfield has an amazing forgiveness meditation. It can seem almost impossible to forgive yourself for certain things. However, using *Willingness* and *Openness,* you can start the process with this exercise.

Start by saying these words to yourself (either silently or out loud). "There are many ways that I have hurt and harmed myself. I have betrayed or abandoned myself many times through thought, word, or deed, knowingly or unknowingly." Allow yourself to feel your body, both physical sensations and emotions. Recall and acknowledge the ways in which you have hurt or harmed yourself. As you bring these memories to mind, accept any feelings and sensations while breathing in a deep, slow manner. Let yourself feel the sadness related to this and give yourself permission to release these burdens. Do this for each of the ways you have hurt or harmed yourself, one by one. Then tell yourself, "For the ways I have hurt myself through action or inaction, out of fear, pain and confusion, I now extend a full and heartfelt forgiveness. I forgive myself, I forgive myself." (See jackkornfield. com/forgiveness-meditation/. You can also find meditations for the forgiveness of others and forgiveness of those who have hurt or harmed you.)

Chapter 9

Mindfulness and Motivation

In this moment, there is plenty of time.
In this moment, you are precisely as you
should be. In this moment,
there is infinite possibility.
—**Victoria Moran**

Remember Susan? These are her words from chapter one: "I love my work, but I feel like I'm drowning. I'm so tired from working all the time. I don't like how I look, how I feel . . . and I can't get motivated to do anything different. I KNOW what to do … I'm just not doing it. I feel so guilty, because I know it's up to me. But it's not getting any better - it keeps getting worse." Susan understood her problem as a lack of motivation. As you may have realized, while motivation is a part of AWESOME, there's so much more to having the life you want.

We typically define *Motivation* as "the general desire or willingness of someone to do something." Synonyms for motivation include enthusiasm, drive, ambition, initiative, and determination. Finding *Motivation* is a common issue, whether it's at work or at home. The real problem is understanding how we create *Motivation*, and whether we need to feel motivated to take an action. *Determination* is one of the synonyms listed above, and it's the most useful for getting in gear.

If you want to get motivated, the fastest way will be to decide to take an action, and then follow through on the action. This is using determination—you are committing to something. This also utilizes *choice*. Instead of thinking about what you *should* do, think about what you *choose* to do—and why. Susan found enormous freedom in this idea. When Susan began to realize that it wasn't a matter of self-flagellation ("I should do this . . . but I don't feel like it—and therefore, I'm doing the wrong thing") and instead started giving herself the opportunity to make a choice, she was able to use determination to see the action through.

It is easier to follow through with a planned action when you don't rely on having the emotional interest in starting. This is why you hear people say, "Think Nike and just do it." Whatever the task is, *start it*. You don't need the emotional experience of motivation to begin taking action. Action requires a commitment to *doing*, which is a straightforward cognitive process. Here's how: go ahead, raise your right arm. Now put it down. You didn't have to delve deep into your motivational psyche to take that action. You read it and did it. (If you didn't—that's ok. You get the point.)

We can get so caught up in our thoughts—"I don't feel like it," "I'm not in the mood," "It's too hard"—that *we stop taking action*. Determination, or making a deliberate choice to act, turns this around. It can also be helpful to start with a small, perhaps unrelated action first. Stand up for a minute, take a walk to the bathroom and back, and maybe take a few deep breaths. Those are all *actions,* and a little movement can set you back on track. There's also a great yoga pose called "feet up against the wall" that can rejuvenate you really quickly and start you back on the path of *Motivation* by determination and choice. Here's how you do it: Lie on the floor with your lower body close to the wall. Raise your feet and rest them on the wall. You can spread your arms out to the side at about 30 degrees. Take a few breaths—nice, slow, deep breaths. Focus on your breathing and *stop repeating the endless loop of why you don't want to do anything.* In a minute or two, go ahead and get up (this is truly the hardest part, since it can be a little awkward).

Neuroscience and Motivation

Neuroplasticity has given us some cool insights about building *Motivation* as well. When you use your pre-frontal cortex (the thinking part of your brain) to plan an action, your brain starts to release the excitatory neurotransmitter glutamate. Glutamate neurons are involved in learning and the formation of memory. Glutamate helps in creating *Motivation* by activating dopamine neurons (dopamine is the neurotransmitter that is part of our internal reward system). Dopamine helps you to take and maintain action. Firing up glutamate activates dopamine, which puts you on the reward-motivation pathway. Therefore, just by mentally planning to take an action, your brain begins to reinforce that action with positive, feel-good neurochemical changes in your brain.

Even better, when you plan an action and follow through with the action, the glutamate-dopamine pathway is strengthened. The next time you go to take the same action, you get a little release of anticipatory dopamine. This helps you in following through (and continues to strengthen the pathway). Over time, we rewire our brains by creating new neural pathways through repetition. You have probably encountered this when you are trying out a new lifestyle behavior or activity. Think back to learning how to ride a bike. Chances are it took a bit of practice (repetition) before you were speeding down the sidewalk on your bicycle. Once you learned? Well, that's where we get the phrase, "It will come back to you. It's like riding a bike." You created a bicycle-riding neural pathway in your brain (there are actually a lot of different pathways involved, but we are simplifying this for our example). If you haven't accessed that pathway in a while, it may have gotten a little weaker, but it's still around. Start riding again and it comes back to you. So we best increase the positive feeling of *Motivation* (enthusiasm, drive) by starting to engage in the behavior. Short version? Making a decision (determination) and choosing to act equals increased positive feelings of … *Motivation*!

Mindfulness—Why This is a Must-Have

We've determined that you need to use determination and choice in order to access and increase *Motivation* for your desired behavior. Realistically, how do you put this into action? As you may have gathered from the previous section, you need to be solidly in the present moment in order to enact this procedure. You can't be focused on what happened previously (guilt or other negative feelings about what has gone before), and you can't be anticipating what *will* happen (anxiety or fear regarding the future outcome). You need to be living in (and focused on) what is happening *now*. It is in the present that you are able to alter your neural pathways. You can't go backwards and imagine a different outcome, nor can you go forward and create the future through imagining it into being. I love this quote by Rick Hanson (*Hardwiring Happiness*): "You can manage your mind in three primary ways: let be, let go, let in." It's your opportunity to "let in" and create the life you want to live.

Although we discussed the enormous impact of *Spirituality* in chapter seven and we will look more deeply at *Energy* and related perspectives in chapter ten, you live in the present moment. In fact, we all live in the present, because in each moment that is all we can do. We can't go backwards in time or jump forward in time. We live in a continuous present. It is our attempts to focus on the past or the future which disrupt our thinking and emotions. "Unease, anxiety, tension, stress, worry—all forms of fear—are caused by too much future and not enough presence. Guilt, regret, resentment, grievances, sadness, bitterness, and all forms of non-forgiveness are caused by too much past, and not enough presence" (Eckhart Tolle).

Mindfulness is defined in the dictionary as "the quality or state of being conscious or aware of something" or "a mental state achieved by focusing one's awareness on the present moment, while calmly acknowledging and accepting one's feelings, thoughts, and bodily sensations, used as a therapeutic technique." Thich Nhat Hanh says, "Mindfulness shows us what is happening in our bodies, our emotions, our minds, and in the world."

Dan Siegel (author of *The Mindful Brain*) talks about learning to be aware, not just of what we are actually doing, but to also be aware of how our mind thinks and affects us. Another mindfulness expert, Sharon Saltzberg (author of *Real Happiness*) describes mindfulness as being aware of our thoughts and actions *without judgment* and from a place of peace in order to create room for *insight*.

Three themes come to mind as I read these various descriptions: non-judgment, attention, and present moment. That's the bottom line of *Mindfulness*. Whether you are washing the dishes, working one-to-one with a client, or creating a spreadsheet for an upcoming presentation, *Mindfulness* involves being fully in the present (not worrying about the past or anticipating the future), bringing your full awareness to the current activity, and *doing so without judgment*. In many ways, it is the third component that is so difficult for us to put into practice. We may be fully engrossed in what we are doing, completely in the *now*, and yet as soon as we add judgment into the mix, we have lost our *Mindfulness* practice. Judgment is attached to emotion and reactivity. Judgment leads us down the path of wishing we had behaved differently (focus on the past) or trying to control a preferred outcome (the future). Most of all, judgment lacks compassion.

What is fascinating about judgment is the literal definition versus the common usage. The definition of judgment is "the ability to make considered decisions or come to sensible conclusions." Sounds entirely reasonable, right? And yet when we look at the common operational definition of judgment, it is closer to some version of: "This is bad or good. A weighing of the relative worth of the action, thought, or person" (my definition, not the dictionary). In fact, the verb *judging* is "to form an opinion or conclusion about." And that's exactly what we do, regarding validity, or worth. We form an opinion or a conclusion about a person, a circumstance, an action *as if* it reflects the intrinsic worth. *Mindfulness* requires taking the judgment out of the equation. This is neither good nor bad. It just is. Remember how often people would say, "It is what it is." Did that annoy you? I know a lot of people who visibly recoiled when someone would use that phrase. I generally heard *it is what it is* from someone who was taking a fatalistic (and often covertly judgmental) position in regard to a situation. And yet, few things could be more grounded in the present, and true, than simply stating, "It is what it is."

Effects of Mindfulness on Your Daily Life

The research on mindfulness continues to grow. There are a multitude of studies on the beneficial effects of a *Mindfulness* practice related to your daily life. In many ways, mindfulness has become a buzzword—a fashionable manner of discussing the latest *must-do* trend. And yet, there is significant research about the positive impact of a mindfulness practice:

> *Decreased heart rate*
> *Normalization of blood pressure*
> *Deeper breathing*
> *Reduced production of stress hormones,*
> *including cortisol and adrenaline*
> *Strengthened immunity*
> *More efficient oxygen use by the body*
> *Decreased inflammation in the body*
> > —Deepak Chopra
> > (chopra.com/articles/7-ways-meditation-can-help-you-reduce-and-manage-stress)

The American Psychological Association (APA) has published numerous studies demonstrating the positive effects of mindfulness. Among them are stress reduction, reduced rumination, increased focus, improved working memory, decreased emotional reactivity, increased cognitive flexibility: insight, morality, and intuition, as well as better immune functioning, increased well-being, increased information processing speed, increased relationship satisfaction, and decreased distractibility.

Specific studies regarding health benefits? Fewer migraines, fewer skin rashes, less teeth grinding, less chronic pain, less back pain, fewer symptoms of Post-Traumatic Stress Disorder (PTSD), additional grey matter volume in the brain (specifically in the areas related to emotion regulation), improved ability for relaxation, increased social connection, self-love, empathy, compassion, and kindness. Want more benefits? Decreased anxiety, irritability, and depression, as well as improved sleep and energy, fewer repetitive and restless thoughts, and better concentration and focus.

Mindfulness translates to real-world benefits. Studies show that with mindfulness practice, elementary students demonstrate greater prosocial behaviors, emotion regulation, and academic performance as well as improvements in mood, empathy, confidence and self-esteem, coping and social skills, attention, and focus. Adolescents experienced lower depression and anxiety, resulting in improved academic attainment (Bennett & Dorjee, 2016). Resilience can be significantly increased through mindfulness while decreasing problem behaviors, attentional difficulties, and anxiety. In other words, *Mindfulness* provides potential for freedom and positive growth in the same way the internet gives us access to information in today's world. Before the advent of the world wide web, we were limited by our access to information. A library's card catalog, or connection to greater information systems (or lack thereof) created boundaries. Literally, we could not know what we did not know or have access to. *Mindfulness* practice functions similarly. We are only limited by our awareness, and implementation, of the effects of mindfulness.

How Mindfulness
Super-Charges Motivation

What exactly is the *Motivation* you are looking to implement? Let's consider motivation for exercise—are you looking to exercise to lose weight, fit into a special outfit, increase your overall health and fitness? The source of your motivation is vitally important. If you are hoping for an outcome that is dependent on an external source (trying to please someone else, stuck in the *shoulds*), it's not going to work. This is the most fragile source, as any shift in how you view the external is enough to kill determination immediately. As an example: I want to attract someone's attention, and I think I need to lose weight in order to do this. I maintain a rigorous workout routine until I discover that the object of my affections is completely unavailable. I am disheartened and move into thinking, "Why bother? No one will ever want me." End of exercise.

Short-term motivation (e.g., I want to wear my new bathing suit on vacation next month, so I will give up sugar between now and then) has mixed results. Sometimes the goal is important enough that we stick with the behavior (which is moving it closer to a personal, internally motivated source). More often, the target outcome seems far enough away that we engage in intermittent behavior, because it's challenging to stay motivated and on track for external, short-term goals. As in—I ate no sugar for the first three days. Then I encountered two birthday parties, a night out with the girls, and a visit from my mother-in-law. Cutting out sugar was relegated to tomorrow (and then vacation arrived before I knew it).

Lasting results come from internal motivation that is in alignment with your values and beliefs (I want to stop eating sugar because I feel better and healthier when I don't have sugar). What really matters to you is where you spend your time and energy (other than what you give away to worry and fear). Your choices demonstrate the intrinsic value of your actions. *Mindfulness*, staying in the present moment without judgment and experiencing what is happening, allows you to achieve the satisfaction that comes from matching your values to your choices and behavior. All we ever really have is the present. When we are aware of *what is* instead of focusing on *what isn't*, we are using *Mindfulness*. Bringing *Mindfulness* into your daily life allows you to use determination and choice (and the resultant neurotransmitter pathways) to increase the feeling of being *Motivated* — to increase the enthusiasm and drive with which you pursue your internally meaningful goal.

Exercise—Try This:

There's a particular kind of mindfulness practice called "loving kindness meditation." This is a form of meditation that research shows is helpful with increasing feelings of positivity, love, joy, contentment, gratitude, hope, kindness, and caring to others (Salzberg, 1997; Frederickson et. al, 2008). This meditation is also referred to as "metta" meditation—a meditation that is centered around unconditional love for all beings.

Sit down in a comfortable place where you are free from distractions. Take a few slow, deep breaths. Imagine yourself as a young child (or you at any age—picking a picture of yourself that you can address with unconditional love and support). Repeat to yourself the following words three times:

May I be filled with loving kindness.
May I be safe from inner and outer dangers.
May I be well in body and mind.
May I be at ease and happy.

Now think about someone in your life who has shown you love and compassion, someone you know cares deeply about you and your well-being. As you picture this person, repeat the following words three times:

May you be filled with loving kindness.

May you be safe from inner and outer dangers.

May you be well in body and mind.

May you be at ease and happy.

You can continue this practice picturing other loved ones, friends, or mentors, considering each one at a time and repeating the above four statements. Don't worry if you aren't immediately filled with an everlasting feeling of peace and contentment. This is an individual process, and truthfully—it takes as long as it takes. You are starting with yourself because you need to feel forgiveness, love, and compassion for yourself before you can completely experience these feelings for someone else.

Bonus Exercise—Try This:

Once you have gotten a good sense of the loving kindness meditation as directed to yourself and to those you love, respect, and cherish, try expanding the meditation to include a larger circle. You can imagine your community, your workplace—you can extend this out to the entire United States or to the whole world.

After practicing metta for yourself, those who hold important positive relationships in your life, and expanding your love and compassion to a greater group, comes the biggest challenge. Follow the steps above while you bring to mind someone who has hurt you, harmed you, or who you find to be a difficult challenge in your life. Repeat the loving kindness meditation while imagining this person you associate with negativity or distress. You may experience a lightening or lessening of negativity right away, or it may take substantial practice before you notice a change. Using the *Awareness* you have developed and *Openness* to the outcome, envision doing the metta meditation and feeling peaceful and calm. Although the timing of results is individual, the research results are clear — this helps.

Chapter 10

Energy

We are all connected;
To each other, biologically.
To the earth, chemically.
To the rest of the universe, atomically.
— Neil deGrasse Tyson

Connecting to and utilizing both your personal energy and the universal energy in our world adds the final dimension to the AWESOME process. *Energy* can be difficult to explain (and to understand or accept), and yet this is the unifying force underneath and between everything. In the last few decades, Western society has gradually opened to a variety of healing modalities, generally grouped under the category of "complementary and alternative medicine" (CAM). In fact, the growth of CAM practices has increased to the point where in 1998, a branch of the National Institute of Health (NIH) was created—initially the National Center for Complementary and Alternative Medicine, it was re-named in 2014 as the National Center for Complementary and Integrative Health (NCCIH).

In 2002, the National Health Interview Survey showed that 36 percent of American adults utilized complementary health. One-third of American adults used at least one form of complementary health—which included massage, acupuncture, chiropractic, herbal medicine, meditation, biofeedback, deep breathing, qi gong, yoga, imagery, Reiki, and homeopathy. This is not an extensive list, and even NCCIH could not come to agreement about everything that falls under CAM. Ultimately, NCCIH divided CAM approaches into five categories: alternative medical systems, mind-body interventions, biologically based treatments, manipulative and body-based methods, and energy therapies. The survey also inquired about prayer—and when prayer was added to CAM approaches, the result was that 62 percent of Americans 18 years old and above used some form of CAM practice regarding their health and well-being.

As the use of CAM practices has grown, there have also been advances in quantum physics, psychoneuroimmunology, and a variety of other scientific discoveries. Along with this, there has been a rise in awareness and the practice of *Energy* as a treatment for physical, emotional, and spiritual wellness. In 2012, the American Psychological Association began approving continuing education credits for courses in energy psychology (specifically courses and workshops related to Emotional Freedom Technique (EFT)—"tapping" on acupuncture points, which are on the meridians, or lines of energy, within the body). Mindfulness meditation and Eye Movement Desensitization and Reprocessing (EMDR—bilateral eye movement) are also included under energy therapies. The Association for Comprehensive Energy Psychology (ACEP) defines energy psychology as a "collection of mind-body approaches for understanding and improving human functioning ... focuses on the relationship between thoughts, emotions, sensations, and behaviors, and known bioenergy systems (such as meridians and the biofield). These systems and processes exist, and interact, within individuals and between people. They are also influenced by cultural and environmental factors."

ACEP has collected research information on over 100 different studies, reviews, and meta-analyses from peer reviewed journals (which is the "gold standard" in scientific publication), representing information from over 12 different countries. What's the point of all this? More than 75 percent of the studies showed a significant, large effect. One particular example refers to Thought Field Therapy (TFT, which is the original "tapping" approach) — the Substance Abuse and Mental Health Services Administration (SAMHSA) has determined that TFT is effective for the treatment of post-traumatic stress symptoms. Shortest possible version? We still don't know a lot (from the perspective of scientific "proof") about energy healing, but it works.

"Disease results from an imbalance or blockage in our body's vital energy. By removing the blockage or stimulating the flow of energy, our body can naturally heal itself" (Deepak Chopra). *Energy* healing is a way of understanding the mind-body-spirit (or mind-body-energy) system, which includes connection and communication between our neurobiology, our electrophysiology (internal electrical systems), our consciousness, and our thoughts, behavior, and emotions. Our knowledge of this comes initially from ancient and indigenous healing frameworks that include the meridians, chakras, and biofields: our *energy centers*. Yoga, qi gong, acupuncture, and

Reiki are all healing/wellness practices that have been developed around the body's energy flow.

Yoga utilizes concentration, meditation, breathing, and physical poses to increase relaxation while helping to "balance the mind, body and the spirit" (NCCAM, 2011). Reiki (which means "spiritually guided life force energy" according to the International Center for Reiki Training) involves healing through the use of energy transmitted from the Reiki practitioner to the client using specific hand positions that "free up" the internal flow of energy. A multitude of studies have shown that Reiki helps with stress, pain management, and relaxation. The International Association of Reiki Professionals (IARP) conducted a survey of hospitals that were ranked as the top 25 hospitals in 2002 by U.S. News and World Report. 60 percent of these top 25 hospitals offered some kind of Reiki program. All of hospitals surveyed that used Reiki said they thought Reiki was at least somewhat beneficial for patients, and more than two-thirds of those hospitals described Reiki as highly beneficial. Chances are, if you check out major hospitals and healing centers in your area, you will find Reiki available (often for cancer patients, but increasingly for other patients as well). A study by the American Hospital Association named the top three complementary treatments available in hospitals as massage, music/art therapy, and Reiki.

Music, or sound healing, is another energy practice. Music operates on the part of our brain that involves emotion, and has been helpful in decreasing stress and depression, as well as relieving pain. You've probably seen the effects of music throughout the course of your life. Some music makes you want to move and dance, other music may be relaxing—you may even find some music to be unsettling or anxiety-producing (I've been known to turn off the car radio at times when the beat is too fast, or out of sync with how I'm feeling. This is especially true if I'm feeling stressed or anxious, since it seems to work me up). I've witnessed hundreds of situations in which people I work with have used music or sound to change their mood and emotional state, either improving or worsening their reactions (think angry person listening to "angry" music—you get someone who becomes even more agitated). Tibetan singing bowls are used for sound healing. Each bowl is tuned to a particular frequency, and the practitioner runs a mallet around the outside of the bowl, producing the sound (similar to running your finger around the rim of a crystal wine glass). Some people use a variety of singing bowls and quartz bowls (all at different pitches) to create a *sound bath*. The music is used to clear and stabilize the frequencies associated with one or more of the chakras (the internal energy centers of your body)

Aromatherapy, while not immediately seen as an energy practice, is "the art and science of utilizing naturally extracted aromatic essences from plants to balance, harmonize, and promote the health of body, mind, and spirit" (National Association for Holistic Aromatherapy [NAHA], 2010). Aromatherapy is included here because of the research that demonstrates aromatherapy has been useful in alleviating pain, anxiety, and agitation (as well as a variety of other physical and emotional conditions). This is another area you've probably encountered. Think about the smells you associate with feeling positive or uplifted. There's a good chance this includes some type of a citrus smell. While the exact one may vary (you might like lemon, grapefruit, sweet orange, or tangerine best), there's an almost universal positive response to the larger citrus family. I routinely diffuse citrus scent in my office as a way of setting the mood for progress, positivity, and hope.

Bruce Lipton, Ph.D., a stem cell biologist, bestselling

author (*The Biology of Belief*), and researcher in epigenetics (changes in our genes that happen without changes in our DNA), brings together quantum physics (the invisible realm of energy) with biology. He describes the quantum energy field in the same way as spirit. "The new physics provides a modern version of ancient spirituality. In a Universe made out of energy, everything is entangled, everything is one." Gregg Braden, another best-selling author (*The Spontaneous Healing of Belief*) widely acclaimed for "bridging science and spirituality," details the importance of understanding the way energy works in our life. "We're beings of energy with the capacity to tune our bodies and share particular kinds of energy. When our thoughts direct our attention to a sight that we see, words that are spoken, or something that we otherwise experience in some way, our physical selves respond to the energy of that experience."

Here's an example of how you can recognize the *Energy* forces in your life. Think of a time when you walked into a room of unfamiliar people. As you began to interact and move around, was there someone you immediately felt drawn to? Conversely, have you had the experience of meeting someone and wanting to back as far away as possible, because something about the other person just turned you off or didn't feel right? What about a situation in which you felt compelled to take an action, even though it didn't make logical sense?

This happened to me not long ago. I was in my office building late in the day, and an unknown man stopped by to ask me something. It was a short interaction—I couldn't directly help him but gave him some suggestions, and he left. I heard the front door of the building close and I continued gathering up my belongings to go home. There were still other people in the building, and I completed my regular end-of-the-day routine. As I began to drive home, I had the thought that I should have checked to ensure the man left the building. I dismissed the thought, as I'd heard the front door close and no one was in sight when I left. The further away I drove, the stronger the feeling became. I couldn't shake the thought that the man was in the building, despite no evidence to the contrary. By the time I was almost home (it's a short drive), I felt absolutely *compelled* to return. My husband drove back with me. We went into the building and, after looking around, found the man hiding in a supply closet. This time he really did leave (we watched him, locked the other doors, and notified the police). Nothing further happened, and he hasn't been back since.

This story isn't about the man or the security of my building (although we did start locking the supply closet after this incident). This is about the knowing, the absolute certainty, I experienced during my drive home. There was no logical reason for me to think he was still there—this had never happened before, and I'm not prone to worrying about safety and security in this way. It's a big building, and there are always unfamiliar people going in and out. I use the word compelled because I literally *had* to go back and check. There was no ignoring the thought or the feeling I experienced, despite my attempts to reassure myself or dismiss the concern. This is a story about attunement to *Energy*, and the deep connection and knowing that is possible in our lives. Of course, I can't know what might have happened if I hadn't listened to my inner voice. I can imagine a variety of outcomes, but that doesn't matter.

Joe Dispenza said, "If you practice wholeness as a state of being enough times, it becomes your state of being—and that's when the magic really starts to happen." To me, this was an example of practicing wholeness, regularly walking my talk, and using the concepts and approaches of AWESOME on a daily basis. This is also how we can manifest outcomes in our life. By paying attention to our inner knowing, by using *Energy* practices to align our internal energy centers, and by incorporating *Awareness, Authenticity, Willingness, Wholeheartedness, Engagement, Spirituality, Openness, Forgiveness*, and *Mindfulness* into our life.

Bringing awareness and use of energy medicine into your life is a way to expand your overall health and wellness, connecting the dimensions of mind, body, and spirit. How can you begin to benefit from, access, and use energy in your life? There are several different options. Try going for a massage and, while receiving the massage, allow your breathing to deepen and slow while you focus on connecting to either your internal *life force* or to a sense of spiritual connection with the Universe. You can try a Reiki session, paying attention to any sensations that arise in your body while the Reiki practitioner is clearing your chakras and supporting the best flow of energy through your body. Acupuncture, or acupressure, are also options (generally those are used if you are experiencing a problem, either physically or emotionally, as they function to release blocked energy within your system). Therapeutic grade essential oils are a wonderful support to enhancing mood and concentration. You can find these online or in most health food stores (Whole Foods Market has a great selection). YouTube has thousands of fabulous sound healing clips of varying lengths. Try searching for Tibetan bowls, singing bowls, or just sound healing. You can also find music and meditation that is specific to balancing the chakras on YouTube. Tapping, or EFT resources, are also available on YouTube. Nick Ortner is an invaluable resource and expert in Tapping.

Exercise—Try This:

Bring the palms of your hands slowly towards each

other, stopping about an inch or so apart. Slowly move your hands open and then closer in to each other. Pay attention to what you feel in the center of your palms. You will likely feel a slight sensation similar to the force you feel when two magnets resist each other. It may take a couple tries for you to feel this, but once you do, it's pretty noticeable. This is a way of feeling your personal energy field. As you practice, you can learn to broaden it by first feeling the sensation between your palms and then widening your hands to the size of a ball (or bigger!). You can also watch a video I recorded on this process at youtu.be/yuET6Ye8wrQ.

You can access a talk I gave on energy healing at the 2016 Connecticut Health Expo at youtu.be/Sz4QyXrRThg and my demonstration of a chakra clearing at youtu.be/E8d_czTxqUs. If you are interested in additional uses an types of energy healing, you can search for providers in your local area, or you can contact me at kristinamhallet@gmail.com.

Chapter 11

Where It Goes Wrong

*It is no good getting furious if you get
stuck. What I do is keep thinking about
the problem but work on something else.
Sometimes it is years
before I see the way forward.
In the case of information loss
and black holes, it was 29 years.*
— **Stephen Hawking**

*S*tuck. You're going to be there. If I could realistically promise you something else, something better,
I would. As a child, I was captivated by the idea
that "my word is my bond." I have lived by this maxim
(and quite a few others, because I'm always learning and
growing). As I grew, I internally changed this to something closer to #radicalhonesty. If something is going to

111

hurt, I firmly believe we should acknowledge that reality and tell people, "This is going to hurt, but you will be okay." And that's what I keep thinking of as I write this chapter. You may not know this (actually, you have absolutely no reason to know this, unless you know me personally), but I want *your* life to be easier, for you to learn faster and sooner than I have. I believe that part of my purpose in this lifetime is to be a truth-teller. Someone who will offer a compassionate, yet accurate, blueprint for the obstacles ahead. This is my goal in writing this book, in addition to offering hope and a path forward. But to move forward, you are going to have to negotiate setbacks and obstacles. That's the way life is, and I can't change that. As we've discussed, *you* are the person who is responsible for your thoughts, feelings, and actions. Sometimes it's like watching a movie, when you know the heroine is walking into danger (the music alone is a good clue), and you want to yell at her, "Stop! Go back! Take the other path." And yet, she keeps going forward (because it's a movie, and of course she doesn't hear you).

Why I Wrote This Book (for YOU)

If you picked up this book, then something about the ideas of "burnout" or "motivation" (or maybe the words BE AWESOME!) caught your eye. You want a different outcome in your life. You want to do the things you *know you should* and to live the life you've dreamed of. And yet, it hasn't played out quite that way. You have done the *right* things, worked hard (most likely, you are closer to the perfectionist end of the spectrum and have actually worked *too* hard), and you're not satisfied with how things are going. Perhaps you read *Own Best Friend,* and you've worked to put the "eight steps to a life of purpose, passion, and ease" into play, but it hasn't been *enough*. This is the reason I wrote *BE AWESOME!* In fact, years before *Own Best Friend*, I had started to write this book. At the time, it was called "Being Awesome," and the acronym stood for most of the concepts covered in the *Own Best Friend* EMPOWERS system. Being Awesome was a book I couldn't write and couldn't let go of. I've finally realized that it wasn't yet time. I wasn't ready to move beyond the practical, into the *practical, yet conceptual*. In many ways, I'm still not ready. But this is a book whose time has come. One of my mentors told me "you only need to be two chapters ahead of your clients." Although I was initially appalled (the mostly-recovered Type A perfectionist in me rebelled at this thought), I have since come to see the wisdom in her words. I'm not *there* yet—and I doubt that I will be before I die. Not because I'm slacking or not committed, but because this is a process that goes deeper and deeper. And because life serves us up roadblocks and challenges all the time. Instead, I remind myself that the goal is related to *frequency, intensity, and duration*. If I get thrown off course, or cycle back downwards in the abyss of self-blame and being *stuck* (which will, absolutely guaranteed, happen), my goal is to have this occur with lesser frequency, to last for a shorter duration, and to be of reduced intensity. And that's where I'm proud to say I have been successful. It's not about never making a mistake or never feeling bad— it's about *knowing* that this will happen and modulating your response, so you continue to move forward. It's about having unconditional love for *yourself* as a fallible human being and buckling down to repeat, relearn, and start over again.

Let's say you decide not to *unstick*. What is the likely outcome? The cost to you? I imagine that your dissatisfaction with yourself and your life will grow. You will feel increasingly irritable and experience less motivation over time (and be less likely to act on determination and choice, in the absence of feeling motivation). You may find yourself having increasing difficulties in your relationships (friendships and intimate relationships), primarily because you are on a path to lower self-esteem. You may find yourself being less effective at work, because you are struggling with focus, concentration, and energy. Perhaps you just want to go home and collapse — sitting in front of the television or going to bed because taking care of yourself seems like an insurmountable obstacle. All the while the guilt is growing, as you ruminate on why you can't take the actions you know you *should* to turn things around.

As your physical, emotional, and mental states become more disrupted, you are heading straight for burnout. You can't keep going on your preferred path, and you are starting to fantasize about *giving it all up* and going to work in a shoe department, or at a coffee shop. At the same time, the likelihood of you developing some form of physical illness is rapidly increasing, as your body (physically, mentally, emotionally, and spiritually) is screaming for rest, support, compassion, and to have a break. With less energy, you have greater difficulty keeping up, and perhaps you *believe* your level of achievement is falling (which may not be accurate, since you are no longer viewing yourself objectively). As a result, your self-esteem drops lower, and you begin berating yourself for not doing more. Yuck. What an ugly process! Did it strike a bell with you? And yet, I have described my inner thoughts and journey before committing to #BeAWESOME.

Just as I finished writing this, I received notification of a new email. This was the email message from Dan Pedersen (on *Medium*): "Worrying about what other people think about you, will prevent you from being your best.

It will prevent you from being real. It will prevent you from doing the right thing. It will prevent you from being what others need you to be (which isn't always the same as what they want you to be). It will prevent you from being at peace.

Do what brings you peace. Not only will you be more satisfied, but you'll be what the world truly needs you to be. A peaceful mind creates peace in the world." Isn't that beautiful? And timely? In so many ways (and in the words of Gabby Bernstein), the "universe has your back."

Ellen was one of my coaching clients. She came to me saying, "It's now or never. I need to make a change — *fast*. I feel like I'm sinking, and it has to stop." She identified her primary problem as "not enough motivation" and reluctantly admitted she felt on the "edge of burnout." She had been experiencing increasing anxiety and dissatisfaction with her life, felt *stuck in a rut*, and couldn't bring herself to take action. A friend had recommended coaching, and thus we began. My coaching focuses on *moving forward* and is based on the underlying assumption that you are a whole, capable, competent person who encounters life challenges and ups and down *just like everyone else*. I tend to work with driven professional women who have lost sight of their own needs as they juggle multiple roles and responsibilities in a demanding, fast-paced environment. Perfectionism and achievement are often external goals for these women (which is something I personally understand and continue to address). All too often my coaching clients have been caught in the cycle of high performance leading to higher performance, without maintaining balance. This tends to result in increasing guilt, as they constantly feel they aren't doing enough while also wondering, "What about me?" (and feeling selfish for having those thoughts!).

Ellen began to work through the AWESOME process.

In her case, she started with *Awareness* and *Authenticity*, which rolled right into *Willingness, Wholehearted,* and *Worthiness.* So far, so good. For Ellen, the next step was *Openness* and *Forgiveness.* She had to imagine both being open to new ways of perceiving, as well as moving to *Forgiveness* regarding the choices that had led to the present. As a card-carrying perfectionist, Ellen struggled with *Forgiveness.* It was *so easy* for her to revert to the *I shoulds* and the *I shouldn't have.* She made "simple, not easy" her personal mantra as she worked on her coaching goals, reminding herself that feeling challenged did not equal unworthy or *not good enough.* Like many high-performers, Ellen wanted to move quickly through the process, and she did. AWESOME is not a linear process—it's presented in this fashion for ease of translation. In real life, the components of AWESOME are woven together, and some of the strands repeat more often. It's completely unique, while reflecting the common threads and experiences of all of us.

As an over-achiever, Ellen was *not* happy when she found *Wholehearted, Worthiness,* and *Forgiveness* resurfacing. "I thought I *did* that! Am I *ever* going to get this?" was her despondent query at our fifth meeting. Never mind the extraordinary gains she had made to date. Forget acknowledging the new awareness, authentic living, and improved mood. From Ellen's perspective, this was devastating. And a failure. My response? We assess re-wiring through frequency, intensity, and duration. *Not* perfection. I reminded Ellen that this is ongoing work throughout our life, as we *unpeel the onion,* layer by layer, through facing new challenges and opportunities to grow. "I hate the onion metaphor!" Ellen wanted to be done. I shared this quote with Ellen: "Let go of certainty. The opposite isn't uncertainty. It's openness, curiosity, and a willingness to embrace paradox, rather than choose up sides.

The ultimate challenge is to accept ourselves exactly as we are, but never stop trying to learn and grow" (Tony Schwartz). Ellen gave me a half-grin, rolled her eyes, and then laughed. "I get it. To #BeAWESOME, I have to embrace the journey, because there's no destination until the final one." She got it.

Chapter 12

Moving Forward

*We must be willing to let go of the life
we've planned, so as to have the life
that is waiting for us.*
—Joseph Campbell

We started this journey together talking about Susan (and so many other women) who find themselves in the situation of *knowing* the problem ("I'm not taking care of myself in a healthy manner"), and *knowing* the solution ("Make time to move my body, eat well, and get enough sleep"), but not taking action to address the issue. We identified two central issues, *guilt* (the *I shoulds* deriving from our expectations of ourselves as needing to be more, do more, achieve more, which usually result from some version of *I'm not good enough unless...*); and *simple, not easy* (the reality of implementing change that affects us at the deepest level).

Are you getting the sense that this is an interminable process, that never seems to end? It is, and it isn't. In reality, AWESOME is a process that you will go through multiple times, each time hitting a deeper level of *Authenticity, Wholeheartedness, Openness,* and (usually) *Forgiveness.* As you utilize *Engagement, Spirituality, Mindfulness,* and *Energy,* each area of your self-development will continue to expand. And the life you have imagined will also change, as you explore and encounter new challenges, new opportunities, and new dreams.

When I was a child, I was uncomfortable ordering at a restaurant. I felt self-conscious and had difficulty looking at the server. Eye contact was definitely out (if you know me, this may surprise you, as today I revel in connecting with people and make eye contact and smile at strangers all the time). As a young teenager, I vividly remember being unwilling to call the library to check on the closing time (and this was before caller id, so it was a completely anonymous call). I participated in academics and sports without problem, mostly because I had clear target goals and could demonstrate my worth through achievement. Looking back with compassion, I send loving understanding to the younger me who didn't realize her own worth as a person.

I remember my family praising my ability to "bounce back" from any adversity, although I suspect this was more of a surface response than actual resilience since I took any criticism, *failure,* or disappointment deeply to heart. Often, I would work harder, faster, longer to make up for whatever I didn't do perfectly. I smiled, connected with others, and continued to focus on achievement as a way of feeling good about myself. There's a limited shelf-life to achievement-based esteem, since there's always someone else who is doing more, and doing it better. I would intermittently fall into internal despair, until the next project or goal came along. It's an insidious process, because there's unlimited opportunity to improve—not only is our culture regularly pointing out what we *need* to change about ourselves (lose weight, dress a certain way, attract a certain type of person, have a particular kind of life), but I work in the field of mental health. Self-awareness and personal growth are taught as foundational elements to providing support and assistance to others.

I went to psychotherapy, read books, and talked to supervisors, friends, and family. I tried journaling, attended trainings and workshops, and practiced self-reflection. But it didn't have the soul-deep impact I wanted, because I approached everything in terms of *fixing what was wrong with me*. I didn't start from a place of non-judgmentally knowing and loving myself. And my drive to accomplish and achieve was a combination of meeting (what I perceived as) the expectations of others and hoping to get to a place of self-worth. As if this was a final destination, and as if it depended on a specific achievement or course of action.

This is not to say that I was stagnant. I learned a lot of things about myself and made many changes over this period of time. I had mastered eye contact and smiling by middle school, and my comfort in talking to new people significantly increased during college. I became more comfortable asking questions and for help/directions/service (which required a lot of practice). I learned to be more objective (and not take it so personally) when I received comments and critiques. Graduate school and then working as a psychologist increased my sense of connection to others and repeatedly demonstrated the value in engagement and listening. I'm a natural caretaker, and working to help and support others came easily to me. It also covertly switched my sense of achievement from obvious goals (grades, promotions, etc.) to achievement through being of service to others. Service is wonderful, and I think having a servant's heart is invaluable, but to be most effective, it needs to come from a place of internal balance between caring for others and caring for self. I believe that truly authentic interactions have the most impact, and that requires being able to acknowledge and take care of your own needs, not just everyone else.

I don't precisely know when the shift began. I'm certain all the reading, training, and living had an effect. I know that working with others to feel and live better was a continuous opportunity for self-reflection and made a difference. I had figured out that *Authenticity* was an important personal value to me and realized that I needed to *practice* being authentic to live this value. *Engagement* was already integrated into my life (although if you recall from earlier in this book, my practice of engagement has vacillated over time). The shorthand I use to describe this, in my own mind, is that I committed to walking my talk. It's no surprise that the more I acted upon this, the more successful I was in helping others. *Willingness* and *Openness* were hand in hand with *Authenticity*, because I had to take risks, make changes, and start *stretching*.

At dinner one night with Julie, one of my closest friends, she challenged me to broaden my horizons in the area of food. I tended to eat the same things repeatedly, and trying new food was rare. She had suggested we eat at a Thai restaurant, and I had reluctantly agreed. This was just before New Year's Eve. After we ordered (which I did with great trepidation), she suggested I make a resolution to try new food on a regular basis. Our discussion pointed out one of the ways in which I was living small and holding back. I had never looked at it that way — in my mind, I was sticking with what I knew and liked, which just seemed sensible. This conversation had a huge impact on my life. I accepted Julie's challenge (this is the same friend who gave me a magnet with the saying by Eleanor Roosevelt to "do one thing every day that scares you") and began to actively try new foods. Most of the time this worked really well, and I began to enjoy a far wider variety of foods. Ginger, edamame, and avocado immediately come to mind as current favorites that I would never have tried without Julie's encouragement. In reality, I was allowing vulnerability while practicing *Awareness, Openness, Motivation* and *Accountability*. I find that it's often the little things—the small actions, the minor choices—that create the biggest difference in our attitude and approach. By actively expanding my food palate, I was also learning self-compassion and self-care. When I connected these dots, I was able to shift my focus to the areas of *Worthiness* and *Forgiveness*.

I stumbled into the practice of yoga (going to my first class solely to please someone else). In that first class I had a powerful experience of *Mindfulness* and moving meditation. I was able to quiet my mind from comparison and experience being completely in the moment, with fully bodily awareness (yoga has played an important role in my life in terms of insight—you can read about some of these in *Own Best Friend*). Yoga was also the pathway for my discovery of *Energy* and added a new dimension to *Spirituality*. Throughout all of this, I was learning and implementing new ways of practicing self-compassion and *Worthiness*. This was building a foundation of true belief in myself as a person of worth—not based on accomplishment or achievement, but simply for the person I am. At the same time, I became more able to openly and directly discover and confront my inner feelings of *not good enough*.

Have you ever seen a set of three interlocking rings? (I discovered this is called a Borromean ring. If you Google it, you will see great examples. This is also a design that's used for a number of wedding rings.) All three are interlinked, but if you remove any one of the three rings, the other two are no longer connected. This is my image of how AWESOME works. Each one of the concepts are vital to the whole. If we take one out, the whole structure doesn't hold together in the same way. Using my ring analogy, you can have a series of stacking rings instead, but it's not fully integrated. The Borromean ring demonstrates the way in which we consistently return to the different parts of AWESOME, as our movement in one direction facilitates access to a new portion of a ring we've already worked through. I like this better than the onion metaphor, primarily because this image also allows us to see that we can move in any direction (including backwards), as a matter of choice. Every time I have learned and integrated one part of AWESOME, I am now able to see and approach new areas of the whole. The entire process shifts forward, so there is room for continual growth and discovery.

In chapter five, I told you my karaoke story, and how I stopped being afraid to sing along with "Happy Birthday," releasing old beliefs of being not good enough (and recognizing it is more important to sing from the heart in celebration than whether you sound like an angel). The gains in *Worthiness* (and *Forgiveness*) unlocked new opportunities for moving forward in the greater area of creativity. Along with not singing, I had always carried the belief, "I am not creative." What this really meant to me was that I wasn't artistic—specifically, that I couldn't draw. Perhaps it would be more accurate to say that believing I could not draw led me to believing I wasn't artistic, and thus not creative. Because looking back, that's what really happened. So often the barriers we erect don't just prevent us from further growth, they also close in more and more, so we end up at a place that's even more restricted than where we started.

I came to the clearer understanding of how this happened as I contemplated what I wanted to focus on in the new year. I decided to set an intention to embrace creativity—setting an intention is reflective of how we want to feel and act going forward. In my mind, it's a kinder, more compassionate way of considering (and accepting) who I want to be as my best self. The problem with resolutions is that it's a set-up for seeing yourself as succeeding or failing. A resolution is a commitment, but without the compassionate understanding that as a human, there are going to be bumps in the road. And all too often with resolutions, once you hit a bump and don't make it to the gym, or you eat French fries or have a crappy day at work, then you begin a negative internal dialogue. You know the one—it goes something like, "Ugh, it's only January 19th, and I've already failed at my resolution. I never stick to anything. Why do I even bother setting resolutions? Nothing's going to change anyway." And so, the spiral begins. A resolution is defined as "a firm decision to do or not to do something," while intention is defined as "a thing intended; an aim or plan." An intention is a means of clearly stating your goal while maintaining a compassionate (and likely more realistic) stance towards yourself. Let's face it, doing something 100 percent of the time is hard. And for those of you who are perfectionists, anything less than 100 percent equals failure—and also means you're way more likely to not even try. For example, you might say, "I intend to treat my body in a loving and caring way by going to the gym." Your focus is on how you'd like to act towards yourself, and the gym is one way of meeting that intention. It's also a reminder that if you're not moving your body or going to the gym, you have an opportunity to assess whether you are treating your body in a loving and caring manner. And if that happens, it's a lot easier to say, "Oh yeah, that's right—

the reason I wanted to go to the gym is about treating my body well" and pick up right where you left off (or come up with a different means of meeting your intention). When we set an intention it's an opportunity to envision something that reflects your best self, not who or how you *don't* want to be. And to remember that you are human, and that none of us are perfect. Because being human is about trying, falling, and getting back up with new knowledge to try again.

As I set the intention to embrace creativity, I wasn't sure where this would lead me. I only knew I wanted more *Openness, Awareness* and *Authenticity*. Here's what happened — I started to do an art journaling course led by Brené Brown and Oprah Winfrey. This actually felt pretty good, and I was able to be playful and have fun with stickers and markers. I had the chance to continuously practice non-comparison and non-judgment, in accepting and loving my heart-driven attempts. Feeling emboldened, I agreed to attend a craft night with my friend Jill. Jill is fabulously creative and artistic, and her support (and gentle pushing to keep walking my talk around my intention) convinced me to sign up and go. I wasn't excited about it, but I did feel pride that I was pushing my own boundaries.

The night of the event Jill and I met for dinner. We had a great time, but I noticed that as dinner came to a close and it was time to walk to the event, I was feeling a little anxious. Having worked to increase my *Awareness*, I gave myself a little internal shake and told myself to "get over it—it's no big deal." This wasn't a compassionate self-response, but it's what happened. We walked in and sat down, waiting for the instructor to begin. The task was simple—paint a heart on a piece of barnboard. As everyone got settled, I noticed my leg had started bouncing up and down, a sure sign my anxiousness was increasing. My face must have given it away as well, as Jill asked me several times if I was ok. This time I worked to be kinder to myself and took some deep breaths, reminding myself that change, and challenging our false beliefs, can be uncomfortable and scary. My intellect recognized the task was simple, but my sense of self was ready to flee—to head back to the land of not good enough and comparison.

I kept intentionally breathing and tried to stay in acceptance instead of judgment (which took some work). We began and starting helped me to focus and brought some calm. I painted my board with a turquoise heart, intentionally leaving parts of the inside of the heart undone. This was an opportunity to embrace imperfection. (I later realized the heart was also off-center, an unintentional imperfection. Somehow, that was a little harder to accept.) When I finished, I felt a similar sense of pride and accomplishment to what I felt the night I did karaoke. Despite feeling anxious and slipping towards judgment and staying small, I had persevered with compassion. Different from karaoke, I decided to hang the picture in my office as a visible testament to my loving imperfection and desire to keep moving forward. It's in a noticeable place and is a way for me to illustrate *Worthiness* to myself through action.

It's taken me many decades to move from afraid to call the library to hanging my imperfect art on the wall. Along the way there have been triumphs, setbacks, and times I simply turned in circles without even knowing it. AWESOME is a compilation of the wisdom I've gained through reading, studying, listening, and living. There have been many failures and disappointments, most of which brought me the greatest growth and strengthened my belief in hope, love, and compassion. *Own Best Friend* was the excavation and *BE AWESOME!* is building the well that we can always draw on for nourishment, allowing us to refresh and revitalize, so we keep moving forward. Drink deeply, and love your imperfect self, with compassion and joy.

Notes—References and Additional Resources

Introduction

APA Stress in America Survey www.apa.org/news/press/releases/stress/index.aspx

Jamieson, J., Nock, M., Mendes, W. (2012). Mind Over Matter: Reappraising Arousal Improves Cardiovascular and Cognitive Responses to Stress, Journal of Experimental Psychology, Vol. 141, No. 3, 417–422

Chapter 1

Brown, C. B. (2012). *Daring Greatly: How the Courage to Be Vulnerable Transforms the Way We Live, Love, Parent, and Lead.* New York, N.Y.: Gotham.

Jansen, A. S., Van Nguyen, X., Karpitskiy, V., Metenleiter, T. C. & Loewy, A. D. (1995). Central Command Neurons of the Sympathetic Nervous System: Basis of the Fight-or-Fight Response, *Science*, vol. 270(5236), pg. 644–646.

Schmidt, N. B., Richey, J. A., Zvolensky, M. J. & Maner, J. K. (2008). Exploring Human Freeze Responses to a Threat Stressor, *Journal of Behavior Therapy and Experimental Psychiatry*, vol. 39(3), pg. 292-304.

Seligman, M.E.P., T. A. Steen, N. Park & C. Peterson (2005). Positive Psychology Progress:

Validation of Interventions, *American Psychologist*, vol. 60(5), pg. 410.

van der Kolk, B. (2015). *The Body Keeps the Score: Brain, Mind and Body in the Healing of Trauma*, Penguin Press, ISBN-10: 0143127748.

www.nicabm.com/guilt-vs-shame/ Infographic from NICABM on the difference between Guilt and Shame

Chapter 2

Carr, A. (2013). *Positive Psychology: The Science of Happiness and Human Strengths*. Abingdon, Oxon: Taylor and Francis.

Cuddy, A. J. C. (2015). *Presence: Bringing Your Boldest Self to Your Biggest Challenges*. New York: Little, Brown and Company.

Seligman, M. E. P. (2012). *Flourish: A Visionary New Understanding of Happiness and Well-being* Atria Books, ISBN-10: 1439190763

Sincero, J. (2013). *You are a badass: How to Stop Doubting Your Greatness and Start Living an Awesome Life*. Running Press, 2013, ISBN-10: 0762447699

Seligman, Martin, University of Pennsylvania, Authentic Happiness — www.authentichappiness.org.
A plethora of positive psychology measurements to assess various aspects of happiness.

www.ted.com/talks/amy_cuddy_your_body_ language_shapes_who_you_are

Chapter 3

Brach, T. (2004). *Radical Acceptance: Embracing Your Life with the Heart of a Buddha*. New York, NY: Bantam Books.

Davis, M., Eshelman, E. R. & McKay, M. (2008). *The Relaxation and Stress Reduction Handbook,* New Harbinger Publications, 2008, ISBN-10: 1572245492.

Kabat-Zinn, J., & Sounds True (Firm). (2006). *Mindfulness for Beginners.* Louisville, Colo.: Sounds True.

Mendius, R., & Hanson, R. (2010). *Buddha's Brain: The Practical Neuroscience of Happiness, Love, and Wisdom.* Paw Prints.

Tutu, D., & Tutu, M. A. (2015). *The Book of Forgiving: The Fourfold Path for Healing Ourselves and Our World.*

Chapter 4

Bolier, B., Haverman, M., Westerhof, G., Riper, H., Smit, F. & Bohlmeijer, E. (2013). Positive Psychology Interventions: A Meta-analysis of Randomized Controlled Studies, *BMC Public Health*, Vol. 13, 119.

Brown, B. (2015). *Rising Strong* (First edition.). New York: Spiegel & Grau, an imprint of Random House.

Chödrön, P. (1997). *When Things Fall Apart: Heart Advice for Difficult Times.* Boston: Shambhala.

Mohr, T. (2015). *Playing Big: Find Your Voice, Your Mission, Your Message.* New York: Avery, an imprint of Penguin Random House.

Nht, Hanh, T. N., & Hoopla digital. (2014). *Truly Seeing: Classic Dharma Talks.* United States: BetterListen! LLC.

Siegel, D. J. (2011). *Mindsight: The New Science of Personal Transformation.* New York: Bantam Books Trade Paperbacks.

Siegel, D. J. (1999). The *Developing Mind.* New York: Guilford Publications.

Fredrikson, Barbara — www.positivityratio.com. Offers on-line tools including Positivity Self-Test and

Social Connectedness Test with graph and score tracking of retake results over time; Loving Kindness and other guided meditations.

Siegel, D., TedX Talk - www.youtube.com/ watch?v=J-BJpvdBBp4

Chapter 5

Hanson, R. (2016). *Hardwiring Happiness: The New Brain Science of Contentment, Calm, and Confidence*. New York: Harmony Books.

Kornfield, J. (2010). *The Art of Forgiveness, Loving Kindness and Peace*.

Leaviss, J. &. Uttely, L. (2015). Psychotherapeutic Benefits of Compassion-focused Therapy: An Early Systematic Review. *Psychological Medicine*, 45(5), 927-945. doi:doi:10.1017/ S0033291714002141

Liu, Q., McLaughlin, A.C., Watson, B., Enck, W. & Davis, A. (2015). Multitasking Increases Stress and Insecure Behavior on Mobile Devices, *Proceedings of the Human Factors and Ergonomics Society Annual Meeting*, Vol. 59 (1), pg. 1110-1114.

Neff, K. (2015). *Self-Compassion: The Proven Power of Being Kind to Yourself*. New York, NY: William Morrow.

Tolle, E. (2016). *A New Earth: Awakening to Your Life's Purpose*.

brenebrown.com/the-research/

greatergood.berkeley.edu/article/item/how_to_grow_ the_good_in_your_brain

Neff, K. — www.self-compassion.org. Self-compassion exercises, research studies, self-compassion questionnaire.

Chapter 6

Ainsworth, M. D. S. (1989). Attachments Beyond Infancy. *American Psychologist,* 44(4), 709-716. dx.doi.org/10.1037/0003-066X.44.4.709

Booth, C. L., Rubin, K. H., & Rose-Krasnor, L. (1998). Perceptions of Emotional Support from Mother and Friend in Middle Childhood: Links with Social-Emotional Adaptation and Preschool Attachment Security. *Child Development,* 69(2), 427-442

Emmons & McCullough, M. E. (2013). Counting Blessings Versus Burdens: An Experimental Investigation of Gratitude and Subjective Well-Being in Daily Life, R.A. *Journal of Personality and Social Psychology,* Vol. 84, pg. 377-389.

Hazan, C. & Shaver, P. (1987). Romantic Love Conceptualized as an Attachment Process, *Journal of Personality and Social Psychology,* Vol 52(3), Mar 1987, 511-524

Seay, B., & Harlow, H. F. (1965). Maternal Separation in the Rhesus Monkey. *Journal of Nervous and Mental Disease,* 140(6), 434-441. dx.doi.org/10.1097/00005053-196506000-00006

www.mentalhealthamerica.net/issues/state-mental-health-america

www.ted.com/talks/brene_brown_on_vulnerability

Emmons Lab, UC Davis - www.psychologyucdavis.edu. Summaries of gratitude study findings. Gratitude Questionnaire, GQ-6.

Chapter 7

Brach, T. (2016). *True Refuge: Finding Peace and Freedom in Your Own Awakened Heart.*

Kornfield, J. (2018). *No Time Like The Present: Finding Freedom, Love, and Joy Right Where You Are*. S.l.: Atria Books.

Peterson, C., & Seligman, M. E. P. (2004). Character Strengths and Virtues: A Handbook and Classification. Washington, DC: American Psychological Association/New York: Oxford University Press. Pg. 601

Tedig van Berkhout, E. & Malouff, J. M. (2016). The Efficacy of Empathy Training: A Meta-analysis of Randomized Controlled Trials. *Journal of Counseling Psychology, 63(1)*, 32-41. dx.doi.org/10.1037/cou0000093

Verghese, A. (2008). Spirituality and Mental Health, *Indian Journal of Psychiatry*, 50(4), 233–237. doi.org/10.4103/0019-5545.44742

www.ncbi.nlm.nih.gov/pmc/articles/PMC2755140/ MH and spirituality

www.livinglifefully.com/flo/flobemindfulnessofthismoment.htm

www.viacharacter.org/www/Character-Strengths/Spirituality

www.mentalhealth.org.uk/sites/default/files/impact-spirituality.pdf

Miller, R. — www.irest.us. Yogic deep relaxation downloads and research summaries.

Chapter 8

Jackson, J. J., Hill, P. L., Payne, B. R., Roberts, B. W., & Stine-Morrow, E. A. L. (2012). Can an Old Dog Learn (And Want to Experience) New Tricks? Cognitive Training Increases Openness to Experience in Older Adults. *Psychology*

and Aging, 27(2), 286–292. doi.org/10.1037/
a0025918Title as presented

Kornfield, J. (2012). *Bringing Home the Dharma:
Awakening Right Where You Are*, Shambhala
Publications

Shi B., Dai, D., Lu, Y. (2016). Openness to Experience as a
Moderator of the Relationship between Intelligence
and Creative Thinking: A Study of Chinese
Children in Urban and Rural Areas, *Frontiers in
Psychology,* 7, 641 DOI:10.3389/fpsyg.2016.00641

Sin, N. L. & Lyubomirsky, S. (2009). Enhancing Well-
Being and Alleviating Depressive Symptoms with
Positive Psychology Interventions: A Practice-
friendly Meta-analysis, *Journal of Clinical Psychology,*
vol. 65(5), pg. 467-487.

Rebok, G., Ball, K., Guey, L., Jones, R., Hae-Young, K.,
Marsiske, M., et. al. (2014). Ten-Year Effects of the
Advanced Cognitive Training for Independent and
Vital Elderly Cognitive Training Trial on Cognition
and Everyday Functioning in Older Adults, *Journal
of the American Geriatric Society* doi.org/10.1111/
jgs.12607

Singer, T. & Klimecki, O. M. (2014). Empathy and
Compassion. Current Biology, 24, 875-878.

Williamson, M. (1996). *A Return to Love: Reflections on
the Principles of "A Course in Miracles"*, HarperOne,
ISBN-10: 0060927488

self-compassion.org/the-research/

Chapter 9

Boellinghaus, I., Jones, F. W., & Hutton, J. (April 01,
2014). The Role of Mindfulness and Loving-
Kindness Meditation in Cultivating Self-

Compassion and Other-Focused Concern in Health Care Professionals. *Mindfulness, 5,* 2, 129-138.

Bowden, D., Goddard, L., & Gruzeleir, J. (2010). A Randomised Controlled Single-Blind Trial of the Effects of Reiki and Positive Imagery on Well-Being and Salivary Cortisol. *Brain Res Bull.,* 81(1):66-72. doi: 10.1016/j.brainresbull.2009.10.002.

Braverman, A. & Meiran, N. (2010). Task Conflict Effect in Task Switching, *Psychological Research,* 2010, vol. 74(6), pg. 568-578.

Carson, J., Keefe, F., Lynch, T., Carson, K. et. al. (2005). Loving-Kindness Meditation for Chronic Low Back Pain: Results From a Pilot Trial, *J Holist Nurs.,*23(3):287-304.

Coholic, D. & Eys, M. & Lougheed, S. (2011). Investigating the Effectiveness of an Arts-Based and Mindfulness-Based Group Program for the Improvement of Resilience in Children in Need. *Journal of Child and Family Studies.* 21. 10.1007/s10826-011-9544-2.

Felver, J. C. & Jennings, P. A. (2016). *Mindfulness* vol. 7: 1 doi.org/10.1007/s12671-015-0478-4

Fredrickson, B. L., Cohn, M. A., Coffey, K. A., Pek, J., & Finkel, S. M. (2008). Open Hearts Build Lives: Positive Emotions, Induced Through Loving-Kindness Meditation, Build Consequential Personal Resources. *Journal of Personality and Social Psychology, 95*(5), 1045–1062. doi.org/10.1037/a0013262

Harpin, S., Rossi, A. M., Kim, A., Swanson, L. (2016). Behavioral Impacts of a Mindfulness Pilot Intervention for Elementary School Students, *Education*, v137,2,149-156.

Hutcherson, C., Seppala, E., & Gross, J. J. (2015). The Neural Correlates of Social Connection, *Cogn Affect Behav Neuro-sci.*,15(1):1-14. doi: 10.3758/s13415-014-0304-9.

Olson, K., Hanson, J., & Michaud, M. (2003). A Phase II Trial of Reiki for the Management of Pain in Advanced Cancer Patients. *J Pain Symptom Manage*, 26(5):990-7.

Salzberg, S. (1997). *A Heart as Wide as the World: Living with Mindfulness, Wisdom, and Compassion.* Boston: Shambhala.

Tonelli, M. & Wachholtz, A. (2014). Meditation-Based Treatment Yielding Immediate Relief for Meditation-Naïve Migraineurs, *Pain Manag Nurs.* 15(1):36-40. doi: 10.1016/j.pmn.2012.04.002. Epub 2012 Jun 20.

www.apa.org/monitor/2012/07-08/ce-corner.aspx

www.mindful.org/18-science-based-reasons-to-try-loving-kindness-meditation/

Chapter 10

Brown, R. C., Witt, A., Fegert, J. M., Keller, F., Rassenhofer, M. & Plener, P. L. (2017). Psychosocial Interventions for Children and Adolescents After Man-Made and Natural Disasters: a Meta-Analysis and Systematic Review. *Psychological Medicine,* 47, 1893–1905. doi:10.1017/S0033291717000496

Daniels, V., Daniels, K. & Weltevrede, P. (2017). *Awakening the Chakras: The Seven Energy Centers in Your Daily Life,* Inner Traditions/Bear, ISBN:1620555883.

Edwards, S. (2015). Heartmath: A Positive Psychology Paradigm for Promoting Psychophysiological and

Global Coherence. *Journal of Psychology in Africa,* 25(4), 367-374.

Gilbey, A., Ernst, E., & Tani, K. (March 01, 2013). A Systematic Review of Reviews of Systematic Reviews of Acupuncture. *Focus on Alternative and Complementary Therapies,* 18, 1, 8-18.

Han, S.-H., Hur, M.-H., Buckle, J., Choi, J., & Lee, M. S. (January 01, 2006). Effect of Aromatherapy on Symptoms of Dysmenorrhea in College Students: A Randomized Placebo-Controlled Clinical Trial. *The Journal of Alternative & Complementary Medicine, 12,* 6, 535-541.

Kalla, M. & Khalil, H. (2014). The Effectiveness of Emotional Freedom Techniques (EFT) for Improving the Physical, Mental and Emotional Health of People with Chronic Diseases and/or Mental Health Conditions: A Systematic Review Protocol, *JBI Database of Systematic Reviews and Implementation Reports,* vol. 12(2), pg. 114-124.

Lehrner, J., Marwinski, G., Lehr, S., Johren, P., & Deecke, L. (January 01, 2005). Ambient Odors of Orange and Lavender Reduce Anxiety and Improve Mood in a Dental Office. *Physiology & Behavior, 86,* 1-2.

Metcalfe, J., Gendle, R., & Thomas, I. (1999). *Herbs and Aromatherapy.* London: Brockhampton Press.

Miles, P. & True, G. (2003). Reiki--Review of a Biofield Therapy History, Theory, Practice, and Research, *Alternative Therapies in Health and Medicine,* 62-72.

Parker, C., Doctor, R. M., Selvam, R. (2008). Somatic Therapy Treatment Effects with Tsunami Survivors. *Traumatology 14*(3), 103-109.

Waite, L. W., Holder, M. D. (2003). Assessment of the Emotional Freedom Technique: An Alternative

Treatment for Fear. *Scientific Review of Mental Health Practice*, 2(1).

Salamon, E., Kim, M., Beaulieu, J., Stefano, G. B. Sound Therapy Induced Relaxation: Down Regulating Stress Processes and Pathologies. (January 01, 2003). *Medical Science Monitor, 9*, 96.

www.energypsych.org/?AboutEPv2

www.brucelipton.com/resource/article/the-role-spirituality-worldshift

Chapter 11

Malarkey, W. B., Jarjoura, D. & Klatt, M. (2013). Workplace Based Mindfulness Practice and Inflammation: a Randomized Trial, *Brain, Behavior, and Immunity*, vol. 27, pg. 145-154.

Rakes, G. & Dunn, K. (2014). *The Influence of Perfectionism on Procrastination in Online Graduate Education Students*, Proceedings of society for information technology & Teacher education international conference, 799-803.

www.dignityhealth.org/articles/how-human-connection-can-relieve-stress

www.dailyom.com/

www.deepakchopra.com

Chapter 12

Dispenza, J. (2013). *Breaking the Habit of Being Yourself: How to Lose Your Mind and Create a New One*, Hay House, ISBN-10: 1401938094.

Roepke, A. M. & Seligman, M. E. P. (2015). Doors Opening: A Mechanism for Growth After Adversity, *The Journal of Positive Psychology*, Vol. 10 (2), 107-115.

Grimm, D. L., Kolts, R., Watkins, P. C. (2004). Counting

Your Blessings: Positive Memories Among Grateful Persons, *Current Psychology: Developmental, Learning, Personality, Social*, vol. 23, pg. 52-67.

Scioli, A. — www.gainhope.com. Information on various aspects of hope including related research findings; questionnaires for adults, teens, and children.

Acknowledgments

I believe that every single event in life
happens in an opportunity
to choose love over fear.
— Oprah Winfrey

Having published my first book last year, I imagined this process would be relatively smooth. But in line with one of the primary themes of this book, the book two process was *simple, not easy.* Writing about going deeper requires the exact same personal journey—plumbing new depths and encountering obstacles. Through this I have been reminded of the necessity of strong, loving support—for which I wish to thank my husband, **Tom Coates,** and dear friend, **Jill Donelan.** Your tolerance of my erratic schedule, willingness to read, re-read, then read again, and your unflagging belief has both kept me grounded and lifted me to new heights. My mother, **Sandra Hallett,** never misses a typo or a chance to cheer me on. Encouragement and new ideas are courtesy of my brother, **David Hallett**—thank you both! My inner compass comes from my beloved daughter, **Sandra Hallett**, who continues to astound me with her insight, ability to connect with others, and the amazing gift of her friendship.

As always, I remain overwhelmingly grateful to all who have been willing to share their stories with me. Every day I was privileged to witness inspirational courage,

140

commitment to growth and a multitude of opportunities to "choose love over fear." Special thanks to Kelli, Cindi, Tami, Amy, Erin, Natali, Jennifer, Amy G. and Georgi for sharing your wisdom on living AWESOME. I don't have words enough to describe how much I appreciate you!

Special thanks to the Enfield Barnes and Noble and the Granby Starbucks, who hosted many a writing session, providing me with motivation and inspiration through coffee, connection, and a warm atmosphere!

About the Author

Dr. Kristina Hallett is a psychologist, professor, executive coach, and author of international best-seller *Own Best Friend: Eight Steps to a Life of Purpose, Passion, and Ease*. Dr. Hallett specializes in helping driven professional women do *what* they love, with *who* they love, without stress or guilt. She demonstrates that happiness is a choice—a choice that comes from digging deeply and learning to accept oneself fully as perfectly imperfect.

Dr. Hallett reminds us that living your best life starts with being your *own best friend*. Having implemented lasting changes in her own life, she walks her talk. She inspires women of all ages to shift away from failure, expectations, and obligations into a motivated, functional lifestyle. Grounded in psychological practice, with an understanding based on the latest findings in neuroscience and brain functioning and a heart open to the mysteries of life, she guides her clients into living the life they want. Her warm yet professional approach easily connects with both individuals and large groups. Dr. Hallett is in high demand as an executive coach and speaker as her clients unanimously report increased positivity, action, productivity and inner compassion with concrete steps to change their life, starting immediately.

Dr. Hallett received a bachelor's degree in Biology and Psychology from Wellesley College. She was awarded a Master's degree and a Doctorate in Clinical Psychology by the University of Massachusetts and is a Board Certified Licensed Clinical Psychologist. She has published across a wide variety of venues, from peer-reviewed psychological journals to popular online sites such as Thrive Global and Mind Body Network. Dr. Hallett is fully committed to continuing her own growth. Current projects include co-leading a yoga teacher training and her newly available Own Best Friend Coaching certification program. She is dedicated to spreading her knowledge of transformation widely, so that as many people as possible may benefit and move into living motivated lives of joy and fulfillment.

Thank You

Thank you for reading. I'm thrilled you took this step towards living a fantastic life, banishing burnout. Would you like to get more information on actionable steps you can take right away? Jump onto your phone or computer and type in www.beawesome.com.

On that page, you will find some more advice about how to break through what's holding you back. If you're still questioning whether the AWESOME process is for you (or if you skipped to the end to see what happens), here's a checklist to help you out.

How you can know for sure you deserve to #BeAwesome:

- More than once you've thought to yourself, *I can't do this anymore.*
- You don't think it's burnout—you just feel like *you* don't have the motivation, skills, or talent to achieve your goals.
- You have too much to juggle and not enough time.
- Self-care is a great idea, but not practical in your life.
- You're tired. All the time.
- Your middle name should be "Stress."
- You try to fall asleep, but can't get off the merry-go-round of endless worries.
- You just want to be happy.

Thank You | 145

If you checked at least one of those items, it's time for a change. If you checked three to five items, it's past time. If you checked six or more, hooray! This is *your* time to make a change.

Free Video Class: I have a companion video series that goes with this book. Email me at kristina@beawesome. com and use "AWESOME video" in the subject line.

If you are committed to fully mastering the AWE-SOME process in your life, I'd love to support you and talk to you about coaching and how I can provide assistance on your journey. Go ahead and email me at Kristina@ beawesome.com.

Made in the USA
Columbia, SC
04 August 2018